Front Endpaper:
Shea Stadium,
New York,
April, 1967

1. Dave Cowens and Nate Thurmond,
   Boston Celtics versus
   Chicago Bulls, March, 1975

2. Opening of
Winter Olympics,
Innsbruck, Austria,
February, 1976

Following pages:

3. Start of
the Kentucky Derby,
Churchill Downs,
Louisville, Kentucky,
May, 1974

4. Chris Evert serving,
Madison Square Garden,
New York, March, 1977

5. Juan Marichal
pitching,
training camp,
Casa Grande, Arizona,
March, 1965

6. Start of
the Boston Marathon,
April, 1975

7. Tour de France
bicycle race,
Brest, France,
June, 1974

8. Grand Prix
de Monaco,
Monte Carlo, France,
June, 1973

SPORTS!

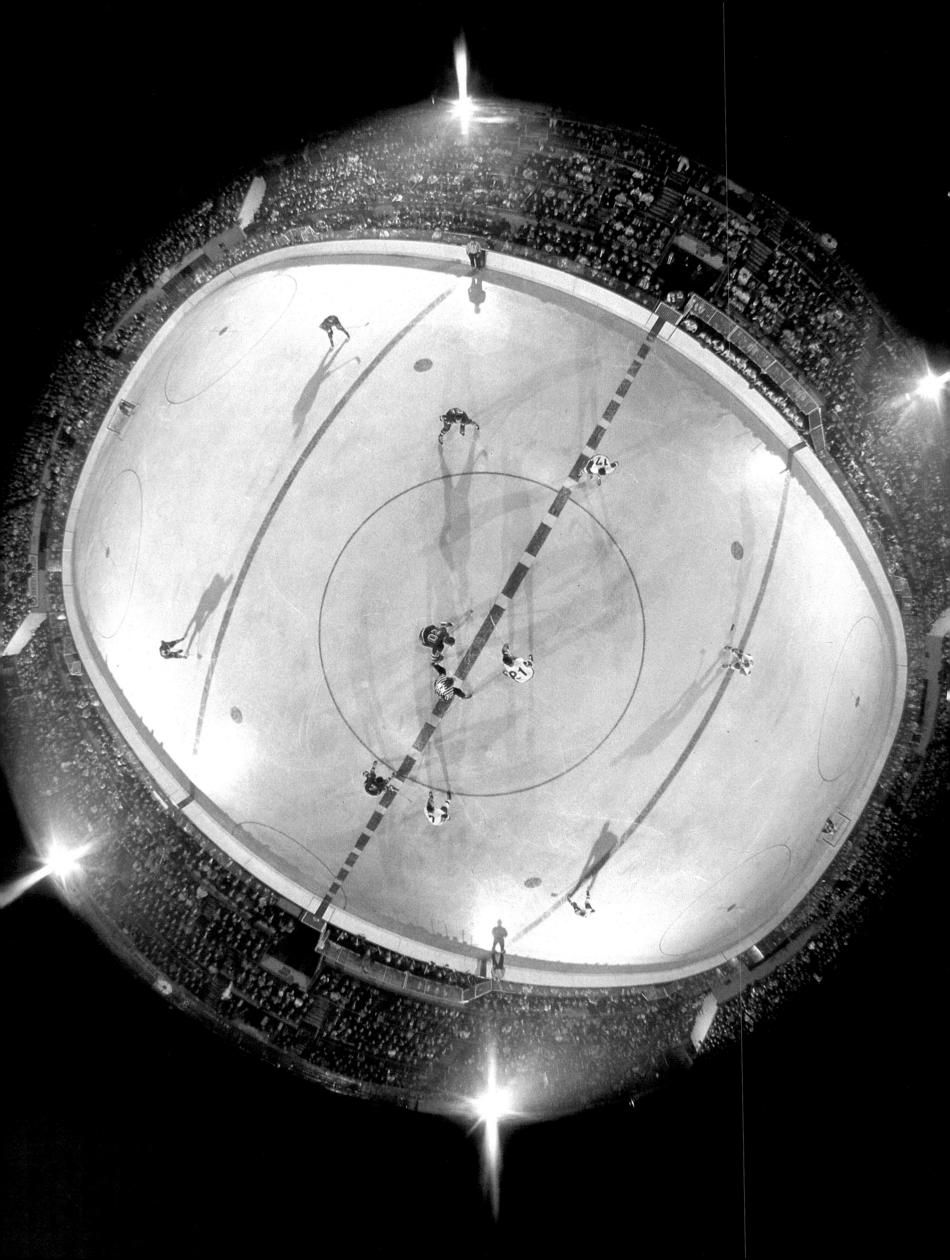

Photographs by **NEIL LEIFER**

SPORTS!

Text by **GEORGE PLIMPTON**

Foreword by **RED SMITH**

Harry N. Abrams, Inc., Publishers, New York

For my mother and father.

Editor: Robert Morton

Designer: Nai Chang

Library of Congress Cataloging in Publication Data
Leifer, Neil.
  Sports!

  1. Sports. 2. Photography of sports. I. Plimpton,
George. II. Title.
GV704.L44   796′.022′2   78-7166
ISBN 0-8109-1631-2

Library of Congress Catalogue Card Number: 78-7166
Text © 1978 George Plimpton
Foreword © 1978 Red Smith
Published in 1978 by Harry N. Abrams, Incorporated, New York
Printed and bound in Japan

CONTENTS

Neil Leifer
Ringside
Benitez - Curry Garden
Madison Square Garden
7-3-78
LeRoy Neiman

FOREWORD

The dictum that one picture is worth more than a thousand words is one of those glib generalities that grow fuzzy when regarded closely, like the image on a television screen. Which picture compared with whose words? It is also said that next to a middle-aged married man, the camera is the greatest liar in the world, and that isn't necessarily so, either. The fact is, the camera can tell a story with smashing impact, and it can deceive.

Consider the picture of Reggie Jackson (photograph 33). The wide and satisfied smile tells us that his bat has made contact, he is still tingling from the shock of the blow, and he knows the ball is on its way out of the park if not the country. Right? Not altogether. The truth is, this was a third strike and he missed.

When it comes to telling a story, much depends on the photographer. He needs technical proficiency, of course, but more than that he needs a plan. He must have a story sense, must know which details are essential to the telling, and he must accept whatever demands of effort and inconvenience are entailed.

The opening picture in this book, New York's Shea Stadium at sunset, offers an example. To get the shot he wanted, Neil Leifer worked from a helicopter. That in itself is no big deal, but it happened that the helicopter's position was smack in the approach pattern to LaGuardia Airport. It wasn't just a matter of hovering at the desired angle, snapping the shutter and getting out of there, for Neil was waiting for the reddening sky to reach full blush. The chopper had to keep moving away to avoid incoming aircraft, returning to hover while Neil tried again.

To tell the story of Frank Shorter's victory in the marathon at the 1972 Olympics in Munich, two pictures were shot from the same position. One shows a horde of runners setting off on their tour of twenty-six miles, 385 yards. The other shows the American finishing by himself. But it wasn't all that simple. The start took place in afternoon sunshine. Two hours and twelve minutes later, evening was coming on, the light was failing and Neil fretted, envying Joshua for his power to stay the setting sun.

There are photographs here taken from the rafters of the Boston Garden and the gondola under the acrylic roof of the Houston Astrodome, by remote control with cameras hung from the ceiling of Madison Square Garden or planted in the middle of a football huddle. To get Dorothy Hamill receiving her gold medal for figure skating in the winter Olympics, Neil perched opposite the victory stand and peered between flags.

He caught Bruce Jenner, the Olympic decathlon champion, just as his victory lap brought him under a big American flag. For the start of the Boston Marathon, Neil worked from the bucket of a cherry picker crane. He shot the start of the New York Marathon from a helicopter over the Verrazano-Narrows Bridge. He rode backwards on the bow of an iceboat in Wisconsin. The plan is indispensable. Before climbing a ladder to photograph Micki King, the Olympic diving champion, he herded a dozen youngsters into the pool because with only water in the background, the sense of height is lost.

Only a few of these pictures are the result of "trick" photography. There is a double exposure with Francis Tarkenton's features superimposed on a blackboard covered with X's and O's—portrait of a thinking quarterback. Shots of Gaylord Perry pitching and a diver's entry into the water were made with a photo finish camera, which stops the action as it flashes past an open shutter.

Still another ingredient goes into photojournalism of this quality in addition to technical skill, forethought, imagination and intelligence. It is luck, and it cannot be anticipated.

As soon as the field reached the clubhouse turn in the Belmont Stakes of 1973, the camera corps moved onto the track and took up positions on the outer half of the course a little below the finish line. By himself, Neil Leifer crossed the track to the infield just above the finish. There was no grand strategy involved; all he knew was that he would be shooting from an angle different from the others.

After three-quarters of a mile, Secretariat left his rivals for dead. When he started down the stretch the others were, literally, still back there across the Queens County line. Then Ron Turcotte, realizing that a track record was within reach, kept the big red colt under a vigorous hand ride all the way to the wire, even though he was winning by thirty-one lengths. As they swept past, the jockey was turned to watch the electric timer on the infield tote board, and he seemed to be looking directly into the camera. He was riding Secretariat to an American record for a mile and a half, and only Neil's camera caught him in the act. Luck.

Neil and Herb Scharfman, another *Sports Illustrated* photographer, were on opposite sides of the ring in Lewiston, Maine, when Sonny Liston took a love pat from Muhammad Ali and lay down to think beautiful thoughts. Neil's picture shows Ali standing over Liston screaming at him to get up and fight because the crowd was shouting "fake." (Which, indeed, the crowd was, intelligently.) Neil's picture shows Ali's contorted face. It also shows Herb Scharfman, a fine photographer so positioned that he can photograph nothing but Ali's rear elevation. Luck.

Speaking of Ali, the portrait, photograph 28, is the view of his exquisite self that he loves best. This is the print he uses when an idolator wants an autographed picture.

To one who has walked the sports beat even longer than Neil Leifer, this book is a gold mine of memories. Here is Sugar Ray Robinson, 45 years old and going on 90, trudging to his corner in defeat after ten weary rounds with Stan Harrington in Honolulu. Harrington wasn't the worst fighter in the world but it is safe to say he never saw a boxer in Robinson's class, because when he was growing up there weren't any.

When Robinson was at his peak, I had occasion to visit St. Louis now and then and I liked to go to the zoo and chat with a black jaguar, a creature of fearful beauty. "Good morning, Ray," I would say. "Nice to see you again." And I could imagine I was in the little training camp in the mountains of North Jersey that Robinson called Cabin in the Sky, watching the champion of the world do his thing.

In those days the feeling was that any time Ray Robinson or Willie Pep was going, we had to be there, because we would not see their like again. It happened, though, that the night Robinson, the middleweight champion, challenged Joey

Maxim for the light-heavyweight title, I was aboard the *Gripsholm* bound for Gothenburg.

There was no domestic radio or television coverage of that bout but in mid-ocean we caught a short-wave broadcast from St. John, Newfoundland. It was a glorious night on the Atlantic but, the radio told us, the heat in Yankee Stadium was almost unbearable. Early in the broadcast, a handsome Swedish woman walked through the small lounge where we were huddled around the radio. She heard a name.

"Shoogar Ray," she said, not breaking stride, "I loov him."

The announcer had a clipped British accent and the Briton's gift for cool understatement: "Robinson is bothering Maxim with a left but without response." It was so unlike the descriptions we were accustomed to hear from Don Dunphy that I wondered whether the announcer was actually at ringside or receiving a skeleton report by telegraph and "reconstructing" the bout in the studio. The longer I listened, the more I suspected the description was warmed over.

Suddenly, between rounds, we heard: "Just a moment! Just a moment! They're substituting the referee!"

"Now I know the bum is faking it," I said. I learned, though. Ruby Goldstein, the referee, had collapsed with heat prostration and Ray Miller took his place. After the fourteenth round, Robinson caved in.

That heat-induced defeat is the only "K.O. by" on his record. Ask him about the match today and he says simply: "I lasted longer than Goldstein."

The photographs reproduced here bring back so many memories that I would hesitate to choose a personal favorite, but if I had to try, the portrait of the late Tom Yawkey would be high on the list. This is one picture more eloquent than words, for it shows the owner of the Red Sox watching his team at play, with a fragment of the action reflected in his sunglasses. This, too, stirs a memory.

It was after a game in Boston's Fenway Park. The stands had emptied, the sweepers had not yet taken over, and up in the rooftop pressbox the newspapermen were finishing their stories. One of them paused, groping for a word, and became aware of a familiar sound, the crack of a bat meeting a ball. He looked down.

Johnny Orlando, the Red Sox maître de clubhouse, was on the mound with a bucket of baseballs. At the plate, wearing spikes, baseball pants and a sweat shirt, was Tom Yawkey with a bat in his hands. Orlando would pitch, Yawkey would swing, and every now and then would come the thump of a line drive hitting Fenway's towering left field wall.

The scene told it all. Tom Yawkey was one of the few club owners, maybe the only one in his time, who was also a real baseball fan. He owned a team not to make money, not to feed his ego, not to get his name in the papers, but because he loved the game.

Now here was the fan who had just seen his team win, standing in his ball park with his clubhouse man pitching while he hit line drives against his wall. Sometimes money *can* buy happiness.

RED SMITH

SPORTS!

This book opens with an overhead shot of two basketball players (Nate Thurmond of the Chicago Bulls and Dave Cowens of the Boston Celtics) shaking hands at center court just before a game...an appropriate introductory picture since it signals—like the twitch of a theater curtain—that the action is about to start.

Actually, Mr. Leifer, the photographer, would be hard pressed to find a handshake in other sports as pictorially dramatic as basketball's. At home plate, baseball managers extend their palms somewhat weakly and warily when they go out to exchange line-up cards and discuss the ground rules of the ball park with the umpires. In the ring, boxers touch gloves after the ring instructions, but as an afterthought and sometimes they forget. Football players shake hands when the coin is tossed at the formal reception at midfield—"Captain So-and-So meet Captain So-and-So"...the ceremony carried on by the Head Referee with all the solemnity of a bishop's investiture—but still, like the others, it is hardly an occasion which sports photographers jostle each other to record.

Nor is the handshake at the end of a competition. Often it does not happen at all. How paradoxical that a basketball game, which begins with such a traditional act of civility, ends with the players turning at the buzzer and trotting off for the locker room without so much as a glance at their opposite numbers. When a handshake does occur, often it is a perfunctory gesture at best, like what happens when two tennis arch-rivals meet briefly at the net at the end of a match. How things have changed! Up until quite recently in the game of court tennis, which is the forerunner of lawn tennis and is still played here and there, the tradition was to salute one's opponent across the net before the start of play, raising the racquet to the chin like an épee and then turning and saluting the gallery. The gestures in today's tennis have evolved alarmingly in the last decade, as anyone who has watched Jimmy Connors or Ilie Nastase would know. Some of these gestures are directed at the gallery, but they would not be mistaken for salutes by anyone except very small children.

Even in the contact sports the handshake is no longer the tradition it was. Only after the deciding Stanley Cup play-off games do the teams line up on the ice for congratulations—and some of the more competitive players even refuse to go through these courtesies. After a football game, it is true some of the rival players, almost lost in the swirl of the crowd spilling out on the field, shake hands and chat, but from the press box they seem as distant and forlorn as commuters meeting at rush hour in Grand Central Station.

Still, traditionally at any rate, the handshake, coming as it does at the start and the end of the game, divides the competitive day of the athlete into three sections—the preparation, the game itself, and the aftermath. These divisions are as distinct as the thirds of the bullfight—what the Spanish call *los tres tercios de la lidia*—or, in more academic terms, the "beginning, middle and end" which Aristotle felt should frame a dramatic event to produce its own proper pleasure. The text which follows has been arranged this way (one can hardly fault the Aristotelean unities). First, the preparation the athletes go through, along with the psychological fiddling and the attendant terrors. This is followed by the game...a look at the athletes during the contests, especially what runs through their minds under the great stresses of competition. I had always thought that perhaps long-distance runners enjoyed a particular kind of sagacity because of the amount of time available to turn the problems of the world over in their minds. I knew a jogger who memorized almost all the poems of W.B. Yeats in a year of running around the Central Park Reservoir. What the more competitive professionals actually *do* think is to be found in what follows. So is something about the "end," or the aftermath, and how athletes compose themselves if things have gone badly, and something about rejoicing too.

I should add that, from time to time, a friend of mine enters the text—quite surprisingly, though what he offers is usually germane to the subject at hand. His name is Timothy Dickinson. In appearance, with his black, frock-like suits, he continues to dress like the English schoolboy he was some time ago. He carries a walking stick. When he shakes hands, he sticks it under his arm. He is a scholar of, among other fields, military matters (their relation to sports intrigues him); he possesses an astonishing memory, coupled with a lively sense of comparison: he is *reminded* of things. He remembers dates. His interruptions will be especially refreshing to those readers who get weary after too severe a spell of sports.

Timothy: "Will there be any more discussion of handshakes?"

"Oh, there you are. No, I think not. Perhaps we have done with that."

Timothy: "Gentility can have alarming consequences. As any schoolboy can tell you, in the Second Battle of Lissa in 1866—in the so-called Seven Weeks War between the Prussians and Italy on one side, and the Austrians on the other—the Conte di Persano closed with the Austrian flagship, *Ferdinand Max,* and badly damaged her. He was urged to ram her and finish her off once and for all, but he refused on the grounds that it was not 'sporting' to do such a thing. A gentleman did not ram another gentleman's battleship unless it was in working order. While the Count was explaining this to his flag officers, he was himself rammed and sunk."

"I see. I was not aware that there was a Second Battle of Lissa," I admitted. "Nor a First. Nor a Seven Weeks War."

Timothy: "The Conte di Persano certainly regretted there had been such an affair. And that he had been taught so much about the civilities."

"Perhaps he didn't shake so many hands after that," I suggested.

Timothy: "He would have had good reason not to."

I

The fields, the courts, the rinks, the diamonds, the pitches, the ovals, the rings, the links—that great variety of playgrounds—elicit the strongest feelings of envy (at least in my case) of those who actually think of those places as their "offices" ...where they go to practice their skills. There are a number of pictures of these arenas in this book—one a high shot from an airplane looking down on a night baseball game, on what the novelist Thomas Wolfe called "the velvet and unalterable geometry of the playing-field." There is one of the Astrodome, gleaming in the evening like a vast U.F.O. come to rest. Alex Karras, the Detroit Lion tackle, once told me that before the visiting team went out on the artificial carpet floor of the Astrodome, a tall Texan dressed like a preacher with a tall beaver hat would appear at the door of the locker room and lecture the team on how it should comport itself on the artificial surface. "They were proud of that Astroturf like it was a fancy Persian rug," Karras said. "This character would call out at us, 'Brethren, I am aware that your habit on your home fields—in places like Detroit and Cleveland, and even Atlanta in the heart of the South—is to spit and urinate on the ground when the urge is upon you. Here, we ain't got that habit.' He'd look at us and raise this long finger. 'There is to be no spitting and urinating on the Astroturf. Offenders will be persecuted to the fullest extent of the Texas law, which means they will be either lynched or shot, depending on whether the citizens or the constabulatory gets there fustest.' "

As such, most ball parks being antiseptic, forbidding places, occasionally their occupants try to bring a touch of individuality to the premises. A black hen lives under the stands in Yankee Stadium. It has been there since a fan brought it to a game in the New York–Cincinnati World Series in 1976 and tossed it out over the railing in the general direction of the Cincinnati bench in the hope of jinxing the Reds who were in the process of sweeping the Series. The fan must have thought his bird more efficacious than a black *cat*, which is usually thrown out in such cases, but the hen turned out to have no power at all: it squawked, unheard in that bedlam, and ran, hippily, helter-skelter before it was swept up by a stadium attendant. The Reds were unfazed. As for the bird, it survived its ignominious performance, and lives in high style under the stands. It is named Moe after the attendant who rescued it, and who cares for it. It lays an egg a day, which is the sign of an extremely contented hen, and when the Yankees are out of town it is given the run of the outfield grass where it moves, a small black surreal shape, pecking in that vast expanse.

There have been other occasional attempts to domesticate the concrete confines of a ball park. Out against the centerfield wall of Tiger Stadium, a tomato plant was grown to quite a respectable height—watered and tended to by the Tiger centerfield, Ron LeFlore—until it was vandalized, purportedly after a particularly poor showing by the club. A similar tomato patch existed in Shea Stadium. Tomatoes, for some obscure reason—perhaps because of their hardiness, or that the grown product is just about the size of a baseball—have always been a traditional baseball plant. The Griffith family, the baseball oligarchy in Minnesota, has an annual contest for weight and size of tomatoes; the ball players bring their entries to the ball park. Cheating is not unknown—a favorite device being to puff out a large tomato with water from a hypodermic; the players carry their prizes gingerly, away from their bodies like waiters with flat bowls of soup; they warn the people grouped around the judging tables to stand back so as not to "bruise" their tomatoes.

The same sort of domestication is much more evident in the locker rooms themselves where in fact players often spend more time than they do on the field.

Bobby Orr, when he was with the Boston Bruins, would arrive at the locker room often five hours before a game. The cubicle areas receive most of the athletes' attention. Satch Sanders of the Boston Celtics tacked the sort of material a house-wife uses to decorate a pantry shelf around the border of his cubicle—scalloped edges it had, and it was pink, as I recall. On his shelf he kept a neat array of lotions, salves, and brushes. A cassette player murmured. His clothes hung neatly from a wooden hanger. His shoes, placed side by side, narrow and very polished, and long, pointed out into the locker rooms. In contrast, next door was Dave Cowens' locker—barren as a packing box laid up on end. When he dressed for a game, he stepped out of his trousers and hung them on top of his shirt like a towel from a bathhouse hook. His shoes lay at angles, one of them upside down. The locker room attendants preferred players like Cowens. They had a lot of mother hen in their personalities, and they liked to pick up after the sloppier players. They would say proudly, "Man, it was like a rummage sale in here a little while ago." When Cowens was out on the court, one of them would set his shoe upright, and put it next to its mate.

The lockers could suggest something of the character of their occupants. I have heard the theory that the lockers of offensive and defensive people on a football team are quite different. The defensive people, whose function on a football field is to run amok and destroy, are messy and they sit on their stools and dress amidst a rubble of belongings; the offensive players, on the other hand, are trained to run exact patterns, as carefully designed as architectural drawings, and their lockers are as neat as pins. They seem to be self-sufficient in character and many of them enjoy hunting in the off-season. They are at ease in the woods. The defensive people are not. They must lash out at things. They play handball in the off-season. Perhaps that's why it used to be said that Notre Dame carried both an offensive and defensive priest.

One of the odder decorations I can remember from football was a bath mat in front of Bubba Smith's nicely messy locker—he was a defensive end—at the Baltimore Colt training camp in Westminster, Maryland. It had two rubbery bosoms rising off it, a sort of anatomical bas relief, and when Bubba stood on it, working his toes, a beatific smile tacked itself on his face as if an oriental back scratcher were being worked between his shoulder blades. The mat had actually been sent to another Colt player by an admirer, but when the big tackle (he was 6'9" and weighed 270 pounds) saw it being unpacked, he moseyed over and appropriated it. No one seemed to mind very much.

As for the messiest, certainly by the end of the season the Detroit pitcher, Mark "The Bird" Fidrych's locker at Tiger Stadium would be in the running—a mare's nest of clutter, much of it bird dolls of different types which fans, to honor his famous nickname, hurl from the stands, often when he is being interviewed on the field. The dolls flutter down, their necks flailing out of the purple and yellow mop-feathers, and hit next to him, inert, as if brought down by a perfect pattern of #4 shot. Fidrych collects them and they overflow his cubicle. John Hiller, who has the locker next door, put down an adhesive tape as a border one summer and mock-warned that if any of Fidrych's "toys" slopped over onto his side, he was going to tear them apart and consume them.

The cosmetic attempts, of course, and the collecting of artifacts and such things take place in the home locker rooms. The visiting locker rooms always have a stark aura about them—there was never anything surprising to find within as the teams walked in from the team bus except perhaps an exhortatory message, half rubbed out on the blackboard, or the chalk whiplash of a play diagram drawn up hurriedly that was supposed to put whatever team had been in there the previous night back into contention.

According to the attendants, visiting club locker rooms were left comparatively orderly by the also-ran teams, who came in with poor records and behaved like country cousins coming to visit and careful not to get mud on the carpet. When they gargled Gatorade they were careful to do so back in the paper cups, or in the sinks, and they lobbed their sucked-dry orange peels with the accuracy of basketball foul-shooters into the center of the trashcan with the onion-skin liner folded back over the sides. The champion clubs, on the other hand, the contenders, came through like tornados—orange peels crushed into the carpet; the splinters from plastic cups crunched underfoot; the players gargled wherever they happened to be at the time, between their bare feet on the rug if they wished; the garbage cans were overturned in the general scuffling and roughhousing after the game; the players wallowed in their celebrations like hogs. Towels were snapped. The showers overflowed. The Canadiens behaved like that. So did the professional baseball and football clubs from Pittsburgh.

To watch the behavior in a locker room is often, of course, to observe an exercise in diversity—especially in the pre-game attitudes of soccer players, who because of their different nationalities and temperaments behave in very different ways. In the New York Cosmos locker room, it was Pele's ritual to lie on the floor with his feet elevated on the bench, a towel neatly folded under his head, another shielding his eyes, and half-in, half-out of his cubicle, he would begin a sort of waking dream that never varied much—Brazilian beaches, and playing barefoot on them, some of the visual playbacks of early triumphs of his astonishing career...essentially a sequence of pleasurable and self-satisfying scenes of his own soccer skills that in his optimistic manner he planned to emulate in the game coming up. The more important the game, the longer he seemed to lie and commune. On the occasion of the first huge crowd the Cosmos drew—65,000 people in New Jersey's Meadow-lands—he spent twenty-five minutes under his towel and then went out and scored three goals against the Tampa Bay Rowdies.

But then just down the line from his locker is Chinaglia, the great Italian striker, whose mental outlook is almost diametrically opposed: he broods like a sour panther; the visions in his mind are of catastrophes...missing shots into an open goal; he will be responsible for the loss of the game; he hears the wrath of the crowd; they are getting ready to bridge the moats that keep them from him. He uses these

29

cataclysmic scenes to work himself into a frenzy to keep such things from actually happening once he steps out onto the field.

On the same team, the great German centerhalf, Beckenbauer, does none of this mental jogging, at least from outward appearance. He is methodical, cool, emotionless, and, watching him, it is impossible to tell whether he is getting ready for a practice or a world-championship game. As he prepares, everything must be just so. Precise. His teammates call him "The Kaiser."

Shep Messing, the free-spirited American goalie formerly with the Cosmos, finds that when he tries the cool, contained approach of Beckenbauer, he fails: his pre-game mood seems to vacillate between the exuberant optimism of Pele ("I'm going to save the game with a last-second leaping grab!") and the plunging despair of Chinaglia ("As I run out to make the last save, I trip and the ball bounces on the back of my neck and rolls along the length of my back into the goal to beat us by one.")

There was not as much praying in a locker room as one might expect—certainly not for victory. Night Train Lane, the great Detroit Lion cornerback, remarked sensibly that there wasn't much point in praying for victory because surely someone in the other locker room would be doing the same. "The Lawd"—if He was at all fair—would realize that the prayers canceled each other out. If there was any praying, it was to ask that one be spared humiliation.

Timothy: "Very sensible...Night Train did you say?"

"That was his name. Train, for short."

Timothy: "The question of praying reminds me of Sir Jacob Astley, who, before every battle (he fought in the Civil Wars) prayed, 'Lord, I shall be very busy today, but if I should forget Thee, do not forget me.'"

"He wasn't praying for victory either," I observed.

Timothy: "Prudence. What *does* go on in an athlete's mind—if one can generalize? What are the manifestations of preparing oneself?"

I went on to say that the butterflies, the tendency to yawn, the staring eyes were all symptoms of preparation. The skiers, as they waited to stand in the "house" with its terrifying threshold that looked down the length of the mountain, yawned, and they peed a lot, drawing little nervous designs in the snow if it was soft enough. "Pee and chew ice," that is what Sugar Ray Robinson did as he waited to be called out to the ring. Others exercised their minds. Charlie Pasarell, the tennis star, would study a notebook he kept up-to-date on his opponents' games. Some were the simplest rituals. Before he set off for a Sunday's game at the Stadium, Tom Matte, the Baltimore Colt running back, always took his dog, Whitey, for a walk in the woods where the two of them would commune; the dog would be informed that Matte was going to have a hundred-yard afternoon; the pair would always end up at the house of a neighborhood psychiatrist where Matte would have a cup of tea and tell his host what the first three plays of the game plan were going to be. (The psychiatrist was always something of a whiz with his neighbors at the game—at least for the quarterback's first series.) Matte always left for the game at the last possible moment. He hated the tension he knew was building up in the locker room. The mood in there affected him and made him sleepy and slack-limbed. So he tried to avoid it.

Some just succumbed to the pre-game torpor. John Unitas often had a nap before a game. So would Jimmy Orr, the Colt wide receiver, who would lie on his back on the training table, stick a long, unlit cigar in his face, and under a towel which hung down over the cigar and his face like a pyramid, he would doze off. Sometimes the tension was such that the athletes were physically sick. Billy Ray Smith of the Baltimore Colts was ill before every game. So was Glenn Hall, the great hockey goalie.

Timothy stirred and said that he would like to say something about tension. When Oliver Cromwell signed the death warrant for Charles the First during the Civil Wars, the tension was such that Cromwell and Henry Marten, one of the other regicides, tried to break it by writing on each others' faces.

"They did what?" I asked.

"That is the historical account," Timothy said. "I don't know *what* they wrote, only that they did."

While I was puzzling over this, Timothy asked if I could tell him something more about prizefighters—after all theirs was the most basic of confrontations, with the considerable lapse of time between fights presumably adding to the tension.

I told him that Muhammad Ali's locker room just before a fight was not unlike what I imagined the *levée* of a French king to be—the fighter craved company; the place was packed; he put on a performance. On the other hand, Sonny Liston sat motionless and peered out of the cowl of his bathrobe. He brooded that the only thing that stood between him and a hot date that night was the man scheduled to meet him in the ring.

"That is Sonny Liston in this photograph?" Timothy asked.

"It is indeed."

"Rather a bully, I would have thought, judging from his expression. One would not be at ease drawing up a chair to play cards with him—especially if you wanted to play Hearts or Go Fish."

"No, I would think not. His costume does not suggest the friendliest of games."

"Go on about mental preparation," Timothy said. "I interrupted you."

I told him that I could only exclaim at the variety and range of mental exercises. When Bill Russell, the great Boston Celtic center, and eventually its coach, first came into the basketball leagues, he spent the hours preceding a game lying on a bed in his motel (one imagines his heels, since he is 6'10", sticking out into the room) preparing himself—which, in his early days, he did by playing imaginary one-on-one duels in his head against the center he was scheduled to face that night, Willis Reed, say. Russell said that the brilliant level of the play between the two as they competed in his mind's eye would make him strain off the bed, the springs squeaking underneath—a sort of Zen game in which neither contestant ever seemed to make an error. The purpose of the exercise, of course, was to get himself ready for the moves he knew Reed was capable of—a form of psychokinetic preparation. Its efficacy began to fade after a while—it was boring finally, and there were better ways of spending an afternoon. So Russell forced himself into other mental catalysts—one of which, he remembered, was to imagine himself as a deputy marshal coming into a Western cowpoke town full of desperadoes—the San Francisco Warriors presumably—and clearing them out in a long sequence of derring-do. Eventually, such mental contrivances seemed foolish, and yet the inability to indulge in them, Russell always felt, somewhat eroded the intensity of his game skills, and indeed signified a time when the game itself would become insignificant. Russell told me about this once—his revelation coming rather abruptly in a play-off game against the Baltimore Bullets in 1969. The Celtics were far ahead, but in the last quarter the Bullets put on a startling rush and began to catch up, much to the wild delight of the partisan crowd in the Baltimore Forum where the game was being played. Russell finally called a time-out to see what tactically and emotionally he could do about holding on to his club's slim lead. His team gathered around him at the sidelines... these familiar faces (no team is as closely knit as a basketball squad—by reason not only of its small numbers but by the length of the season) and they stared up at him, these mates straining to hear him in that welter of sound storming from the stands, trusting in him for some sort of enlightenment. Russell looked down and he suddenly began to laugh. He has a huge rackety laugh: his eyes squeeze shut, his mouth springs ajar, and his face becomes a large aperture out of which emerges a sharp, highly distinctive series of guffaws. His teammates stared at him, thinking that perhaps he had cracked under the pressure of the Baltimore resurgence. Finally, he was able to calm himself down and tell the Celtics what he felt should be done. But he said afterwards that what had happened at the time was a sudden mental realization of the absurdity of what was going on: all the controls, the devices, the mental games to make himself think he was doing something important on a basketball court had collapsed completely; all these gaunt faces, creased with worry, looking up at him were involved in a silly charade. What could be less meaningful than running up and down a wooden floor dressed in green underwear trying to put a ball through a hoop? The absurdity of the sport absolutely overwhelmed him, and he knew that a further, and indeed final, eroding of his competitive spirit had occurred. And although he kept to coaching basketball, that was the last year he played competitively.

Timothy: "It's fortunate that he didn't have this vision of the futility of basketball in, let us say, his *second* year of playing in the league."

"What about generals?" I asked him. "What do they do before battles?"

"Well, General Omar Bradley ordered his staff officers to throw rocks up into the air," Timothy said, "so he could shoot at them with pistols. Why not? He did that just before his offensive in North Africa—pass the time, I would presume."

"And Ike?"

"What's that?"

"What about Eisenhower?"

"Well, you'll remember just before D-Day he prepared two statements. The first said in so many words: 'The landing was successful.' The other read, 'The landing has failed.' He took the blame for it himself. I don't suppose coaches do that—prepare a losing statement."

"I have never heard of one," I said truthfully.

"'We do not consider the possibilities of defeat. They do not exist.' Queen Victoria said that in Black Week, the third week in December, 1899, when the British were having the disasters of Stormberg, Magersfontein, and Colenso. But the commanders are not all as sanguine as that. Commodore Dewey, of course, was violently sick over the side before ordering the attack at Manila Bay in 1898. He needn't have been *quite* so dramatic about it since only eight of his men were wounded in the course of the destruction of the entire Spanish fleet. Or think of General Patton! One would hardly imagine him reluctant to face a fight, but we have the evidence of his nephew, Fred Ayer, that at a dinner party before the general set off for North Africa, he suddenly announced to the assembled company, 'I keep having this dream. I'm standing on the beach at night and washing up with the tide are thousands of dead American soldiers. But their eyes and mouths are alive, and they are shouting, 'Patton, you son-of-a-bitch, you did this to us.' After a moment—the guests all staring at him in astonishment—Patton moaned, 'I won't go.'"

I nodded and said that I was surprised to see certain athletes were able to move out onto the field considering the pressures waiting for them. Take the bullfighter, to pick a formidable example. He wears a cluster of gold medals around his neck. On the hotel room table there are forty-two holy images. He touches each one of them in a prescribed order, and then in reverse. The room is packed with people, but it is very quiet. Nobody bumps into the furniture. Nobody lights a cigar. They stare at the bullfighter praying. The big Hispano-Suiza motorcar is waiting downstairs. When he leaves for the Plaza, sitting in the back seat between two of his banderilleros, the people on their way to the arena will look in the windows and call out, "*Suerte! Suerte!*"

There was nothing he could do to stop what was going to happen. He could not suddenly say, "To hell with your *suertes*. I'm through! Let me out," and the big Hispano would pull up and he'd pile out past the banderilleros, both of them stiff with surprise, and take himself off to a good café. For one thing, before he could reach a café table, the authorities would reach for him and stick him in jail; for another, of course, he would suffer the scorn of his fellowman, that same familiar ingredient of the fear of humiliation in the eyes of his peers that was such a staple of the athlete's consciousness.

Timothy: "Funk. How about your own odd career. Mixing it with professionals. You must have had good enough reason to get out of the Hispano, figuratively, that is."

I said: "The closest I came was when I had got myself into jumping out of a Cessna 180 with a parachute. I didn't like that a bit. But it was a question of not having enough courage to tap the pilot on the shoulder once we'd got up there in the sky and saying, 'Hey, I'm awfully sorry about this, but I've decided to stick with you.

33

It's nice in here. I don't want to go out. I want to go home.' But, of course, I didn't have enough courage to do that, so, whimpering, I jumped. But there have been some with the courage of their convictions," I went on. "In 1918, there was a rookie pitcher named Harry Heitman who played for the Brooklyn Dodgers. He went in for his major league debut and gave up in succession a single, a triple, and a single. He was taken out, whereupon he showered, left the ball park for the recruiting station and enlisted in the United States Navy. 'To hell with it!' he said."

I commented, "I suppose in military matters, Timothy, examples of pure funk are commonplace."

"My goodness, yes," Timothy replied. "In 1921, when the Greeks were invading Anatolia in the Greek-Turkish mess, the Greek commander would claim on his good days that he was made of glass and would surely shatter if forced to advance."

"Glass?"

"The commander may have been referring to himself, or providing a metaphor for his troops," Timothy explained. "I suspect the former. On his bad days, he would simply claim he was dead."

I went on to say that in spirit I thought automobile racing put the most extreme pressures on its competition. On race day, considering what faced them I was surprised that one of the drivers did not drive his car off the grid, onto a country road, and escape. What an equanimity of mind was required!

Jackie Stewart, the former world champion, once described to me what went through his mind as he sat in the cockpit of his car on the grid moments before the instructions to start the engines. He would imagine his body inflating like a "beach ball," and then letting the air out, he would feel himself relax into a slab of slack rubber that seemed to fit the contours of the monocoque...becoming molded inside the racing machine...becoming a part of it...an exercise that not only relaxed him physically, but helped him prepare his mind.

Timothy: "Yes, when Stanley Baldwin made his daily appearance in the House of Commons to pick up the Order Papers—the day's business—he buried his nose in them, absorbing the smell of them with an audible intake of breath, and then he'd plant himself down and crack his knuckles, which he could do like gunshots. It was a ritual that settled him into his day very much like Stewart into his machine. Was the Stewart 'beach ball' trick effective?"

I said that apparently it wasn't. Out on the track Stewart found that his attention began to drift with only a quarter of the race done. He worked at correcting this and toward the end of his career he had developed his powers of concentration so that two-thirds or perhaps three-quarters of the race course would be completed before little snippets of mind-wandering would occur: noticing where a photographer was standing alongside the track, he began speculating where the man might be the *next* time he came around (would he have wandered off?)—almost a game—and his lap times would suffer as a consequence. It was essential to "bite back in" as Stewart says, and he did this by persuading himself that things were beginning to go wrong with his car. A vibration was beginning to develop; how was he going to deal with it? If he eased off, the balance of the car might be affected. He tortured himself with theoretical problems which induced a rapt attention to the matter at hand. His mind seethed. "I'd keep it up, scaring myself," Jackie described it, "so that even if I was winning, it was an ulcer-maker." There is an excellent photo-study of Jackie Stewart in this book, taken as he sits in his car on the grid, waiting, and what is very likely on his mind is that image of that beach ball.

Timothy: "I'm inclined to believe I would prefer the bicycle to the auto if required to race. Incidentally, that is a very impressive picture of the bicycle riders in the book. Your photographer likes to look down on things."

"That is true," I said. "He is always on ladders, or suspended from the rafters."

"I know nothing of bicyclists," Timothy said. "I suppose there is something unique."

"I remember the bicycle riders in Hemingway's *The Sun Also Rises,*" I said, "the French and Belgian racers from the Tour eating supper at long tables in the hotel in San Sebastián. They criticize the Spanish racers for not being able 'to pedal.' I have always wondered about that criticism—it seems somewhat too basic. One of them—I think he's the Tour leader—has a bad case of the boils from the chafing, I would guess, of his rear against those little narrow bicycle seats. He sits on the small of his back. He tells the others, who are all joshing him, that on the next lap of the race he will keep his rear end up so that the only thing that touches his boils will be a lovely breeze. That's the only thing I can remember about bicycling."

"Do they have bells on the handlebars?" Timothy asked.

"I don't know. I'm woefully ignorant."

II

Somewhere amongst Neil Leifer's photographs in this book is a photograph of a diver, the Olympic gold medal winner Micki King, poised high above a pool—an arresting study since the picture has been taken from above (Leifer took it from a scaffolding built above the 10 meter tower) so that King seems to float suspended, as if a hammock has been whipped out from behind her, against the background of the blue water far below. There is something quite ethereal about the picture—the action frozen and composed; the pool, with the boys from the swim club looking up from its surface, is out of focus and soft-looking, cottony, so that the mood of the photograph is that the diver would fall gently toward the water, as if in a dream.

But on inspection, the expression on King's face does not reflect anything like this at all: it is strained, the facial muscles are taut with concentration; intentness and a bit of concern show in the eyes. Small wonder! She is three stories up. She will hit the surface of the pool at 30 m.p.h. The dive is called a "back dive, pike position," what a layman would call an upside-down jackknife. Immediately on her mind is to watch her hands reach and touch her toes. The dive is not a complicated one, but she must work at it. Her hope is to hit "clean," as divers say, producing a ripping sound—"a rip entry"—which spectators will cheer and will be reflected in the judges' scoring. But she is quite aware of a number of untidy things that can happen—from barely noticeable faults that only the judges will catch to major problems of lost control: on occasion a disorientation so devastating can occur that the blue of the sky is confused for that of the water; the diver reaches for it with his fingertips just as, to his numbing surprise, his *feet* hit the water. The possibility even exists of a "balk" or a "change-of-mind" dive—as King describes it—in which everything becomes unstuck and the diver suddenly flails in the sky, seeming to want to climb in the air to regain the board and try again, behaving, in sum, like a cartoon character who steps blithely out of an airplane to discover that he is a mile high.

The antidote to these nightmares, of course, is provided by the sort of concentration visible on Micki King's features. Even after many years of diving she continues to marvel at the speed with which the brain makes the myriad adjustments to correct a faulty dive. In fact, she finds a perfect dive from takeoff to entry almost too easy—okay, so what?—as if the wonder of diving was to put that splendid apparatus to work adjusting and compensating while the body spins and whips in the air. And doing it all in fractions of seconds. After all, diving is perhaps the swiftest sport—short of archery and rifle shooting—in duration of actual activity. Even a put *shot* stays in the air longer than a diver off the low board.

The sort of concentration Micki King focuses on the matter at hand is often so extreme that the athlete remembers little more than the assignments themselves—with no awareness of the crowds or the fanfare or the music or even, in a team sport, the identity of one's opponents. Many athletes remark on how impersonal the action of sport is: opponents become as much ciphers as they are in warfare—a presence, like being aware of troops waiting in a ravine on the other side of the barbed wire. In football, one simply forgot the names of the people across the line of scrimmage. It upset Tom Matte's wife, Judy, to realize this. "But they're your friends...so many of them," she complained to her husband. "How can you not know who they are?"

"I know their numbers," he had said. "We see their numbers in the game films when we prepare for the game; so in the game itself it's always the numbers that we look at. The Detroit Lion linebackers are numbers 56, 54, and 52. Those are the presences I have to deal with when the play starts. I tell myself, '54's moved to where I've got to cut inside him.' They remain numbers until the play is over. Then in the bottom of the pile maybe they become human beings again."

"Well, I should hope so."

"Mike Lucci, the Detroit middle linebacker, says to me: 'You big fat pig! You garbage can!'"

"I'm not sure I like that," Judy said. "Maybe it's better that they stay numbers."

"Exactly," Matte said.

It turns out there is rarely a time when the athletes can let their minds wander. Perhaps the outfielders during a pitching change. Hockey goalies to a certain degree when the puck is being battled for at the opposite end of a rink, especially when a power play is involved and the opposition down a player. The soccer goalie has even more time to let his attention meander. The ball can stay around in the other end for minutes at a time—enough for a goalie to pay a visit to the men's room under the stands and return without incident, and very likely without anyone in the stands being aware. Yet during such moments of inactivity, the professional goalie is supposed to concentrate on the ball—it *can* appear in his area with the abruptness of a twitch. Shep Messing of the New York Cosmos told me that concentrating on the black-and-white diamond ball for the ninety minutes of play, especially if it spent long intervals at the other end, was such an exhausting business that he needed a break from time to time to keep "from going nuts."

"Well, what do you do?" I asked.

He told me that when the ball is out of bounds at the far end, or there is a corner kick down there, he turns around and talks to the goal posts. It gives him a chance to wind down, if only for a few seconds.

"Oh," I said. "Well, what do you say to the goal posts?"

"I joke at them," Messing said. "I say, 'Be there when I need you.' Sometimes I joke with the fans behind the goal posts. They give me advice. I want them on my side."

Such tricks as Messing's were to make one concentrate harder. Eddie Collins, the famous Philadelphia second baseman, always stuck his gum up on the button of his cap when he went up to the plate, but if there were two strikes on him, he would step out of the batter's box to pry the gum loose and pop it back in his mouth: it was the gimmick he used to make himself bear down. Sometimes the ballplayers concentrated by simply focusing almost to the point of madness on what they were *supposed* to do. The intensity in Henry Aaron's mind was such in the batter's box when he hit a home run (even the historic one which broke Babe Ruth's record) that rather than watching the flight of the ball—enjoying what his skill has produced, the way a golfer stares after the parabola of a good golf shot and wishes it would slow down so he can enjoy it more—Aaron turned as soon as he hit the ball and looked down the base path at first base, setting off for it hard, because that is what a player is supposed to do. Too often the ball falls short, and hits against the wall; if the batter has been staring at it, willing it over, he is bound to lose a number of strides on the base paths if the ball stays in play.

Dave Casper, the Oakland Raider tight end, speaks of his mind being so intent on his assignments that he is unaware of even the score, or the passage of time...it is almost as if they must come and lead him away at the end of a game.

Perhaps the most extraordinary example of how concentrating removed the athlete from a general awareness was when Bob Beamon made his amazing 29 foot 2½ inch broad jump in Mexico City. In an event in which advances are made in quarter inches and very rarely, he jumped more than a *foot* over the previous record—the 28 foot range was completely skipped in the record books. The feat prompted the felicitous heading in *Sports Illustrated* that he had jumped into "the next century." But the performer of this extraordinary deed was not aware at the time that he had done anything of particular interest. He hopped out of the jumping pit knowing simply that he had made a *good* jump, and he looked across the infield grass at the scoreboard, where the distances were marked in meters rather than feet and inches, and began—somewhat laboriously because the metric system was new to him—to transpose the figures to see how he had done. The sudden roar of the crowd startled him and he turned to see people emptying out of the stands and coming toward him across the field. He did not know what to make of it. Puzzled, he looked back over his shoulder to see what they were running for—perhaps the winner of a sprint race on the far side of the track—but he saw nothing worth their interest. Then he realized suddenly that they were coming for *him*, arms outstretched, their eyes shining with excitement. Suddenly, he was aloft on their shoulders. It was frightening, he said, because the reason for all this was not set in his mind—as if he were a football coach on the sidelines suddenly hoisted up on the shoulders of his team in the middle of the third quarter and the team down by a touchdown. Beamon kept calling down from the shoulders of his supporters to find out exactly what he had done.

When Timothy remarked that the pleasures of competing must be somewhat diluted by this sort of intensity, I asked if generals had a better time of it in battles.

Timothy said: "Well, Stonewall Jackson was supposed to have said, 'Delicious excitement,' during a particularly savage Union attack. Certainly they are aware of what's going on. By and large I suspect the generals appraise the situation, however catastrophic, and practice being as calm as possible. Do you know what Admiral Beatty said at the Battle of Jutland?"

"No," I said.

"He had just closed with the German Fleet, which opened fire and immediately sank, to everyone's immense surprise, two of Beatty's ships. Just like that. This prompted Beatty to say to one of his officers, 'Chatfield, there seems to be something wrong with our bloody ships today.' He said it in quite the proper form—offhand, collected."

I pointed out that Admiral Beatty's observation could have been said in any number of ways. Perhaps there was no *sangfroid* at all. He could have *shrieked* that line, after all, his eyes bugging out. CHATFIELD! I mean like that.

"Quite unlikely," Timothy said. "Not a Fleet Admiral."

I supposed Timothy was right. But I tried the Beatty line a few times, and by the time I had gone through a number of variations I had forgotten what we had been talking about.

"Concentration," Timothy said. "You were giving examples."

"Oh yes," I said. "Of course."

If concentration was such an important ingredient of the committed athlete's mind (I went on to say), breaking into that concentration was a time-honored ploy of sport. It could be as effective as throwing a spanner into the flywheel of an engine. Baseball had the best-known "bench jockeys" or "agitators" because except for times of stress the game is played in a relative quiet, so that from any part of the park one can clear one's throat at and offer an opinion which will very likely be heard. Old-timers remember two Philadelphia fans—a pair of brothers they were—who sat on the stands on opposite sides of the field, one of them in the upper deck, the other on the third base side, and carried on a shouted and vividly distracting dialogue across the diamond about the visiting player, usually when he was standing in the batter's box getting ready to hit. Their intelligence-gathering apparatus was startlingly efficient. It was one of the mysteries of the baseball world how the two brothers uncovered as much as they did. One can imagine the state of mind of a batter trying to concentrate on a pitch with his peccadillos under discussion between the two— shouted words traveling back and forth over his head like pigeons, about his appearance at the Peek-a-Boo bar, with whom he had been, and what he had been up to afterwards.

The bench jockey the old-timers especially remembered was Jimmy Dykes, who had a voice that whined across a diamond like a buzz saw. "You big busher!" was his favorite descriptive, and he too, like the Philadelphia brothers, had picked up enough gossip to thicken any scandal sheet dossier.

One of the shrillest of the contemporary players is Mark Fidrych of the Tigers, who possesses an hysterical honk-like form of chatter, which is not directed at anyone in particular as much as it is a general effusion of baseball hype, much of it incomprehensible, like a portable radio tuned in between two stations and receiving both. Sometimes the stadium attendant assigned to sit at the end of the bench puts a towel up to the side of his face to blot the sound out, apparently so he can keep his mind in order.

Fidrych is most famous for what he does out on the mound where he practices one of the most common forms of concentration—the self-urging, the near self-flagellation. A television camera zooming in for a close-up often catches him working his lips in a monologue as he fidgets around the pitcher's mound to get things right.

This sort of inner monologue ranges from an inarticulate murmuring to the more discernible patter which would often—as in the case of Fidrych—burst at the lips so that the athlete could be overheard. Tommy Byrne who played for the Yankees in the fifties was perhaps the most voluble of the baseball pitchers. The players had a fine name for him. They called him "The Broadcaster." He'd look down at the batter, his lips moving, and the batter would hear him say, "Gonna throw you a hook, mistah," and sometimes he would, and sometimes he wouldn't. Jim Brosnan, the ex-pitcher author of *The Long Season*, one of the finest baseball chronicles, once told me (he referred to the inner monologue as Silent Screaming) that his thoughts had erupted vocally on one occasion on the pitcher's mound and what the startled batter had heard was *"ils ne passeront pas."*

Of the golfers, Lefty Stackhouse was one of the more expressive. He was famous for admonishing his clubs if they acted up on him, and he would warn the ball down on its tee that if it did not fly out true and far down the fairway he was going to drop it in a pot and boil it.

Timothy: "What do golfers see in their minds?"

I have heard many of them say that just as they hit the ball what they see is a kind of aerial map of the fairway, and what they are thinking is exactly where they are going to put the ball on it, very much as if they were painters leaning forward to dimple the canvas with the white of the ball. "I think I'll put it just *there*." When the ball doesn't go where they see it in their mind's eye, it is a considerable surprise, whereas the average golfer is somewhat surprised to see the ball go where he wishes. I once wrote a book about golf in which I described what crossed *my* mind as I stared down at the ball on its tee. It was that just as my clubhead started down, a large beetle would materialize on the ball. This mental manifestation turned out to be quite infectious; a number of my golfing friends who had made the error of reading *The Bogey Man* bitterly blamed me for a grotesque jump upwards in their golfing handicaps. I was pointed out in the locker rooms as "that beetle man."

Timothy: "I see. What variety of bug or beetle would appear on the ball?"

On a good day (I told him) it might be a midge, barely distinguishable, but invariably the large species would turn up—the grasshoppers, the locusts, the beetles with shiny black backs.

Timothy: "I see."

Perhaps the most involved of the inner monologues (I went on to say) I had heard of came out of tennis. It was practiced by Art Larsen, who was the U.S. tennis champion in 1950. He imagined that he was being advised by an eagle who soared over the court during play. When the point was over, the bird would drift down onto Larsen's shoulder and *whisper* into his ear with advice on court tactics, and what he had noted from above. Larsen was totally absorbed by his device. Spectators sitting in the stands could see the sudden tilt of Larsen's shoulder as the imaginary bird landed, and the slight turn of Larsen's head as he listened to the bird's instructions. He would nod, then, and prepare to serve as the bird took off and soared up to keep an eye on things in the currents at the rim of the stadium.

Timothy: "That's interesting about Larsen. Napoleon apparently had the same aerial view of things on occasion. He once said: 'I foresaw what I might become: I could see the world moving under me, as though I were born aloft in the air.'"

I nodded. "Is that so?"

Of all the games, (I continued) tennis is perhaps the one marked by the steady commentary that seems to go on in the head, usually sharply punctuated by a shout of recrimination at a missed shot. Few who have watched Billie Jean King play have not heard the strident, bitter cry of "idiot!" accompanied by the hard stamp of the foot—too devastating a form of insult to be directed at anyone but oneself. The criticisms thrown at one's doubles partner are apt to be more subdued. One of my father's favorite requests of my mother when they play doubles and she fails to reach a shot is, "Stretch, woman, stretch!"

Some years ago, John McPhee wrote a book entitled *Levels of the Game* in which he set down as best he could devine (from talking to the participants) what went on in the heads of two tennis stars—Arthur Ashe and Clark Graebner—as they played the semi-final match in the first U.S. Open championship on a particularly hot day in 1968 at Forest Hills. As it turned out, both players carried on typical inner monologues, with Graebner's the more traditional. Ashe, McPhee discovered, often drifted into a daydream during a match in which he would think primarily of food, parties, places he has been, and girls, whom, he disclosed to McPhee, he dated in three colors. In the Graebner match he began daydreaming in the second set (he was down one set already) about food, in particular about what he considers the ideal dinner: fried chicken, rice, and baked beans, and it was only by a forceful act of will that he was able to rearrange the priorities in his mind and settle down to the match, which he eventually won. Ashe said he had to work considerably harder to drive such wayward thoughts out of his mind than he did to run down a cross-court shot. No wonder Perry Jones, the southern Californian tennis mentor, always told his players, "Hit the ball and don't think."

Jim Brosnan once told me that he never truly learned to pitch until he learned to stop thinking. If a pitcher's mind was nagged by the tragic consequences of what *might* happen—the long hit—he was doomed; so it was necessary to block such things out, like "turning a valve" as Brosnan described it: the pitcher's concentration should be totally involved in the task of delivering the ball to a particular spot.

One of the tricks that many athletes used to help keep their minds in order during competition was to sing—it helped keep them calm. Jack Nicklaus found that a single song, hummed in a flat monotone, would stay with him through a golf tournament. He told me once, "We won an awful lot on 'Please Answer Me My Love.'"

Chris Evert, the tennis player, also sings to herself—disco rock usually, but only when she has an easy match. If she is extended by an opponent, she stops singing, and begins to remind herself how wonderful it is to win, and what the pleasures of it are, and then conversely, how she will feel if she loses—that she will not only let herself down, but also her family, her friends, and even "the flag" (as she says) as if a loss were close to a national disgrace. She pumps herself thinking of the disparity between these two possibilities—like a bog one must avoid.

Al Feuerbach, the Olympic shot-putter, found that singing commercials put him in the proper frame of mind. Apparently the unusual problem about putting the shot is that since it's impossible to throw any kind of weight off a rigid set of muscles, the competitor must combine a sudden tremendous kinetic explosiveness with the ability to relax: thus as he gets ready Feuerbach's head resounds with ditties extolling the virtues of bathroom cleansers, detergents, and toothpaste—all this his method of trying to get his physical apparatus just right.

The lengthiest vocal efforts are performed by the long-distance swimmers. They go through a quite different sort of mental process since the technical side of the sport is simply to pull oneself through the water until one flops up on a distant shore. There are no tactics. The only mental energy is involved in trying to deal with the slow deprivation of the body's energies. Diana Nyad, the swimmer who excels at this pastime, provides herself with a number of counting exercises and songs to keep herself going. For long stretches she will count every stroke—600 of them to make up a mile—but she relies more on singing songs. On an ocean race off Argentina, between Sante Fe and Correndo, by her reckoning she sang the song "Row, Row, Row Your Boat" almost ten thousand times. After doing this sort of thing for a while, a kind of suspension of the senses takes place—not surprising considering the tedium of the physical activity and the numbing chill of the water—and what Diana calls "night dreams" begin to impinge. During an English Channel swim she became convinced a barbed wire fence had been laid down parallel to her line of direction and that the currents were pushing her into it; she found herself shying her body away from the barbs she was sure would prick her. Further on, she imagined she was being attacked by sea gulls; she treaded water and swatted at them. The support team in the attending boats accepted her plight. It would obviously undermine the swimmer's confidence to tell her that she was imagining things and slowly sliding into lunacy—so they attached towels to oars and waved them, and looked up into the sky and shouted, pretending to deal with a flurry of sea gulls as best they could.

Actually, in the ocean sometimes it *was* hard to distinguish between what was real and the figments of the "night dreams." On the Argentina swim a sea lion joined Diana and swam the last part of the race with her, sliding around her, and over, occasionally approaching her from the front and peering at her gravely above his whiskers, and when she landed, he came up alongside and touched his flippers to the beach. Hearing her tell about it, and how she could feel him graze her body, the people in the boats would have glanced at each other with raised eyebrows and thought it an hallucination like the sea gulls had they not seen the sea lion themselves.

Timothy: "What about horse racing. What are the jockeys thinking?"

I had been in touch with Eddie Arcaro (I told him). He had said: "Your mind is very active—after all, the usual race lasts for just a few seconds over a minute. But since most of the thinking has been done beforehand (figuring out the strategy and where you should be) the mind during the race reacts to impulses in a way that is almost instinctive. You don't tell yourself what to do as if you were reading out of a textbook. In the race you compare what you have decided might happen with what *is* happening, and you make adjustments accordingly. You think: Now this horse should be coming back to me at this point. No, no, you don't look at the horses. All horses' asses are the same. You look at the colors the jockey is wearing. That provides the recognition."

"Oh yes," I had said.

I had asked Arcaro if he had any affection for the horses he had ridden—I mean did he go out to the barns and feed them sugar and scratch them behind the ears and talk to them the way Elizabeth Taylor talked to Pie in *National Velvet.*

He was scornful. "I have affection for their ability. I had affection for Citation, not for him personally but for how he could run. The handlers, the trainers, they're the ones who can tell you about a horse's character and whether he liked to have his ears scratched. I know a horse only to get on him. The day in the life of a jockey—with maybe seven races to ride—isn't long enough for affection."

Timothy wanted to know about the two-legged runners—especially the distance runners. I described what Marty Liquori, who may very well be the best miler of the decade, told me he had on his mind as he runs: "In the first lap the most important thing is staying relaxed, making sure my breathing is right; my diaphragm has to work smoothly, like the bellows you use to blow fire with. I'm not really worried about my position. At the beginning of the second lap, I usually have a false tiredness. If I hear a fast time, I think, gee that was too fast, and I'm tired because of it. If I hear a slow time, I think, gee, I must be awful tired for going so slow. So I compensate by thinking of all the 15-mile runs I took through the snow, and the 20-mile runs on the beaches, and how much tougher *that* was, and it makes me feel better. The third lap is more of the same, except that position is becoming vitally important. I know that going into the fourth lap I have to be in the top two, three, or four—in position and ready to strike. Then, on the last lap, especially the last 300 yards, I try to get mad. I keep telling myself, get mad, mad, mad. It's like slamming a car door when you get so mad you don't care if the window breaks when you slam it. On the last straight it's just a matter of guts. I concentrate on lifting my knees, and hoping the strength I got from all those practice miles is enough."

Frank Shorter told me that marathon runners usually talk for the first third of the race. When I remarked that the idea of *chatting* with anyone at the eight-mile mark, or whatever, was beyond comprehension, Shorter replied that anyone who could not talk easily after running that distance could not consider himself a marathon runner.

"What do you talk about?" I asked.

"It tends to revolve around the race," he had said. "Gossip. If someone goes by us too fast, his elbows swinging, we might remark to one another that there's *one* guy we don't have to worry about. Or we'll talk about some guy who did a lot of jostling about a mile out."

Still, even in distance running, concentration was necessary. Jim Beattie, the first man to run a sub-four-minute indoor mile, once told me what can happen if a runner lets his mind wander. Running in Leningrad in a Soviet-American meet he began thinking about when and where he was going to eat that night—perhaps not surprising being a stranger in that city—and when he focused back on the race he had the sensation of being detached. He spoke of his mind "shorting-out;" he began observing himself from afar, remarking to himself on how well he was doing, and how strong he appeared...so completely absorbed in woolgathering that suddenly he could not remember whether or not he had heard the bell signaling the start of the last lap—extraordinary since the bell is loud enough to pierce through the roar of the crowd to the upper reaches of the stadium. He told me, "I had to turn to Jim Grelle, who was running just off my shoulder, and ask, 'Jim where are we? Is this it?' Jim looked a little surprised (I mean a mile run isn't the best forum for a chat), but he said, 'Yes, it is,' and I said, 'Thank you.' I went into my kick and pulled out ahead five yards before poor Jim had a chance to react. If he'd had the wit to tell me we had another lap to go before the bell, he could have produced *his* kick and he would have soared by me. No, you really have to keep your mind on things."

Timothy speculated: "You couldn't let your mind wander in the bullring, could you?"

"My God, Timothy!" I said. I tried to show off: "Joselito turned his back on a bull, one of the widow Ortega's bulls, in the arena at Talavera de la Reina on the 16th of May, 1920—every Spanish schoolboy knows that date, just as they know the name of the bull who killed Manolete at Linares—and he walked away to look up at the crowd. But that was because he thought he had fixed the bull, not because he was thinking of what to have for supper that night. Of course, he hadn't fixed the bull. It was a misjudgment. It got him killed. The bull came for him, quick and silent. He must have heard the warning scream of the crowd, but there wasn't time to turn. He went up on the horns. He was gored in the lower abdomen and he ran for the infirmary trying to hold himself in with his hands."

"And the name of the bull?"

"I was afraid you'd ask that. I don't know. I looked up the date the other day. But I remember the name of the bull who killed Manolete—Islero, he was a big, grey Miura. But I have forgotten the date. We could call up someone."

"Any Spanish schoolboy."

III

Timothy: "What do they think about when it's over?"

I said it varied. Sometimes it was mundane but appropriate. When Gumba, the Sherpa mountain climber who had stood next to Jim Whitaker on the top of Mount Everest, was asked at a New Delhi press conference what was running through his mind up there on the top of the world, having just conquered it, he smiled slightly and said, "How to get down."

Of course, the reaction depended largely on victory or loss. One of the odd traditions of baseball is that following a loss the players troop in to sit in front of their dressing cubicles, facing in from the stool or bench, and, whatever the size of the score, they observe ten minutes or so of deep mourning. The showers drip in the stalls. No one stirs. Only the attendants move noiselessly and carefully amongst the players, like orderlies in an intensive care unit. Everyone is involved—even those ballplayers who have had nothing at all to do with the outcome and have spent an easy afternoon in the bullpen perpetuating their suntans. *They* are required to observe the ritual, and I have always imagined that at the last out, as they come through the bullpen gate and start walking across the outfield grass toward the clubhouse, they groan to themselves, "Oh man, now I've got to go in there and *mourn* for awhile."

The other sports do not seem to evoke this post-partem attitude after a loss—at least to such a degree. Basketball players, while they may throw a towel or two around, seem to pull themselves together quite quickly. They manage to talk to each other in the shower. A football club, especially if the score is lopsided and the outcome never in doubt, behaves very much as if it had come in from a practice. No one on the squad feels that anything he could have done would have changed matters. A close score, of course, and the self-recrimination and the sour feeling are more evident.

But nothing like baseball. I remember paying a call to the visiting locker room (or clubhouse as it is referred to in baseball terminology) at the Yankee Stadium where the Boston Red Sox had just filed in after losing a game to the New York Yankees in the heat of the 1977 pennant race. It had been a thrilling game—full of excellent plays, and interesting managerial maneuvering, such a good game that the crowd had hung around in the stands, relishing the feeling and trying to store it somewhere, so afterwards they could pull it out, like the contents of a drawer, and refresh themselves with what they had seen. I hoped to talk to Bill Lee, the Red Sox pitcher, who was a lively spirit, and insightful about his profession. He saw me standing at the door of the locker room and waved me over. As I walked by the rows of silent backs, everyone facing into the backs of their cubicles and grieving, I felt very much as if I had been summoned up the aisle of the funeral of a popular high school senior. Though he had not been involved in the game, he was very excited about what had happened. But it was difficult to talk in that atmosphere of gloom.

I whispered, "Man, this club is taking it very hard."

Lee said that the obeisances would go on not only in the locker room, but in the bus ride back to the hotel, and the flight to Boston. No laughter. Lively conversation was frowned on. Certainly no *music* which was a relief in a sense because ordinarily the cassettes and portable radios were turned on in the back of the bus, and the thud of disco rock made the nerves of a sane man, sitting up front trying to read the batting averages in *The Sporting News*, jangle like the string of a banjo. He was reminded that Phil Linz, the Yankee shortstop, had played his famous harmonica on the bus in the parking lot outside Comiskey Park after a loss to the White Sox—famous because Yogi Berra, the manager then, had flown into a rage and got the Yankee management to fine Linz $500.

If you covered baseball, you heard any number of such stories. Gene Mauch, the Philadelphia skipper, once came into the locker room after a particularly depressing loss to Houston, and discovered three of his players enjoying shrimp and barbecued ribs off a spread set up by the visiting clubhouse attendant (Houston was actually the first club to establish what is now a practice throughout the league) and Mauch was so upset to see an example of physical appetite taking precedence over self-indignation that he turned the table over with a roar and with such violence that the barbecue sauce sprayed into one of the stalls and ruined the suit of Wes Covington, the Philly first baseman. Mauch was somewhat embarrassed by what he had done (he gave Covington $100 to buy himself a new suit) but he had made it clear that fingers were not to scrabble around in the shrimp until the proper fealties to custom had been observed.

Of course, though it was more pronounced and traditional, the Coventry-like silences imposed by losing were not restricted to baseball. Lionel Aldridge of the Green Bay Packers once began to sing on a plane trip back from a loss to the Los Angeles Rams. He had a couple of beers and burst into song. Coach Vince Lombardi heard about it, and at the Tuesday team meeting he laced into the team, Aldridge in particular, with such vehemence that suddenly a team revolt began—

Aldridge straining forward with two Packers trying to hold him back, and Bob Skronski, the team captain, shouting at Lombardi that all of them were sick of his kind of verbal abuse. It was only by cleverly shifting the tables and telling his team that *this* was the sort of spirit he approved of that the coach was able to save the situation.

Timothy: "Your description of the baseball players sitting in front of their cubicles reminds me of the Roman Senate when the Gauls captured Rome in 390 B.C. The Gauls entered a city completely abandoned except for the Senate, who sat unmoving—grieving, most likely—in their chairs of state. Indeed, the Gauls looked in and mistook them for statues. The story goes that when a Gallic warrior began stroking the beard of one of the Senators, marveling that such a likeness could be made of wood, the Senator bestirred himself abruptly and cracked the Gaul over the head with his staff—whereupon the Gauls massacred the lot."

I winced. "Let us talk about celebration," I said.

Timothy: "You'll remember that Wellington said that the only thing to compare with the melancholy of a battle lost was that of a battle won."

"I had forgotten that," I said truthfully. I remarked that celebrating in sport was also often qualified since the essential factor was invariably selfish—the degree of exuberance depended entirely upon one's own performance. Jim Hudson of the New York Jets after their astounding victory over the Baltimore Colts in the Super Bowl sat amongst his celebrating teammates bemoaning a tackle he had failed to make on the Colts' Tom Matte. Actually, he wasn't missing much since on that occasion, the ingredients for celebrating were not in evidence. Coach Weeb Ewbank of the New York Jets and Milt Woodard, the president of the American Football League, felt that champagne presented a bad image, that television viewers, especially children, should not watch athletes guzzling down the stuff. So the Jets celebrated their great Super Bowl victory with Cokes and Gatorade. Joe Namath was furious; he said later that it had taken him all evening to wash the taste out with Scotch whiskey.

Perhaps, Ewbank and Woodard had a point. I remember during the Celtics' celebration of victory over Milwaukee in the 1971 championship that Paul Westphal had his first alcoholic drink. Champagne had been provided in the Celtics' locker room. Westphal, whose young, scrubbed California looks suggested total abstinence up until then, decided it was as good a time as any to indulge for the first time—and he did so. It did not take more than two or three draughts from the upturned bottle to turn him into a near-parody of the lamp-post-leaning sot. His exuberance became extreme. He reeled around the locker room. His vocabulary became reduced to "we're number one," and finally to "one," a waving finger upraised. Finally, just as the team was boarding the plane in the Milwaukee airport for the trip back to Boston, he was ill, uncontrollably, his strength drained from him so absolutely that he had to be propped into an airport wheelchair and jockeyed aboard the plane. He had not recovered by the time we reached Boston. He was wheeled out onto the ramp to greet the welcoming crowd, his head lolling forward on his chest, his hands folded in his lap—looking quite like an ancient millionaire being wheeled out of a clinic.

The loudest of the sports celebrants—it has always seemed to me—are yachtsmen. They come ashore from the regatta, perhaps subconsciously relieved to have survived the elements, and they set down their sail bags and wander into the post-race cocktail party where they rock back and forth on their heels and shout happily at each other. The roar spills out of the clubhouse windows. The only comparable decibel level might be reached by golfers, who come off their lonely vigils on the course to describe in great detail what happened to them at the edge of the water hazard on the twelfth to someone who invariably at the same time is explaining what happened to *him* when he was trapped on the third. There is a great amount of talking at a golf tournament party and not much listening.

I am told that marathon runners talk enormously after a race. They have shared a common experience. But the conversation is low in volume compared to the yachtsmen and golfers. They are tired, for one thing, though they are very anxious to recount what they have been through. They sit and drink beer and soft drinks to replace the depleted glycerin and they listen to each other for hours—providing a sound track to accompany the visual memories of the long, quiet struggle they have just completed.

Inevitably, winding down for the athlete meant dealing with the fans. They were always a part of the aftermath, standing in the cement wall corridors outside the locker room doors with the guard sitting on the foldup chair outside to keep them out, or they waited outside the stadium, jammed in against the wire mesh of the parking lot fence with the scraps of paper poked through, with the stubs of pencils, and the pleading cries, so that invariably the tableau reminded the athletes on their way out to their cars of a rather frantic monkey cage waiting to be fed. The athletes had different attitudes about fans' requests for autographs. Some, especially the rookies, seemed to feast on writing out autographs—it was an act that solidified their status—and when they were done with writing out their names for one group they looked around for more. On the morning of a game they sat in the hotel lobbies, their legs stretched out in front of them, keeping their muscles loose and looking very blasé and cool in the hope that the schoolboys moving nervously among the potted palms with their autograph books would recognize them as athletes. They developed their signatures. Johnny Mize, the home run hitting first baseman, drew a circle over the *i* of Mize, like a finishing school girl's affectation, and I did it myself for a while (Mize was a great hero) until the teachers at school stopped it. They said the circles threw them off when rows of them appeared in a page essay on Sir Walter Raleigh bringing tobacco back from the New World; it did not make any impression on them when I said that Johnny Mize dotted his i's that way; they didn't even want to know who he was.

The fanciest autograph I ever saw was Richard Petty's, the auto racer, who if he had a couple of extra seconds to sign would produce a tremendous scrollwork of curlicues and pen swoops into which his name almost disappeared...so that to find it was like looking for the tiger in a *trompe l'oeil* children's book puzzle illustration: it leapt out finally, and the reader would see it suddenly, and say, "Oh, *there* it is."

Mel Ott, the New York Giant, had about the handiest name to jot down in a schoolboy's autograph book, and the worst, or one of them, would be Arnold Schwarzenegger, the body builder.

I would have supposed that actually the easiest to sign would be the signature of the great Japanese home run hitter, Sadaharu Oh.

Here it is, quite tidy, and right up there in brevity with Mel Ott's.

Timothy: "I see."

A curious example was Muhammad Ali's (I went on). He had a very flowery and gracious hand when he was signing Cassius Clay—the c's and s's gave him something to work with and the signature had a certain elegance. His present name, while longer, has little flair when he writes it for a fan. Perhaps the freight train of m's and those vowels, with the squat little caboose of Ali at the end, does not lend itself to much: the fighter scribbles it quickly and reaches for another scrap of paper to sign.

Bill Russell of the Boston Celtics was famous for not giving any autographs at all—not ever—not to anyone he did not know personally. He was frank and polite about it. When the kids raced for him in the parking lot outside the Boston Garden, holding up their pencils and their books, with more coming along behind, yelling back over *their* shoulders that Bill Russell was in the lot heading for his car, he would stalk through them saying, "I don't give autographs," and they would fall away from him, unbelieving. The Celtic management tried to get him to relent in the name of public relations, but Russell was adamant: he felt that the amenities of giving something of yourself to someone, even when it was something as insignificant as signing a name, was reserved not for complete strangers, but for friends. It watered down the value of everything if you were indiscriminate.

"I don't suppose military men are called upon for this sort of thing very often," I asked Timothy.

"Autographs? No, but I can think of one who would have had his work cut out for him: Admiral The Hon. Sir Reginald Aylmer Ranfurley Plunket Ernle-Erle-Drax. He fought at the Battle of Jutland."

"It would be unlikely he shortened it to Reggie Drax," I said.

"Very," Timothy said.

The adulation of the fan—whether seeking autographs or not—could be threatening. In Italy, when Jackie Stewart was the world champion race car driver, the crowds made life for him at the racetracks an exercise in furtiveness. On race day he traveled to the track in a helicopter, not only for convenience' sake but because he could set down in a secluded place where he would not be hemmed in by fans. He was spirited into the pit area like a piece of contraband. After the race he was hurried into the Ford-Tyrell van, his team clustered about him like a rugger scrum. Once he was inside, the fans circled the van, the ones in back leaping to catch a glimpse of him at the windows. Inside one felt the camper begin to shudder slightly, the shock absorbers groaning underneath, and one knew that hands or even bodies were being pressed up against the aluminum sides with people pushing from behind, so that the adulation became almost a corporeal presence. The camper rocked. The drinks tilted in the glasses. Outside they yelled "Jack-ee! Jack-ee! Jack-ee!" without letup, while inside, the team sat around the star, a slight figure with his black Scotch miner's cap, and chatted uneasily, the way children whisper during a sharp thunderstorm and hope it goes away.

I remember sitting next to Red Auerbach, the Celtics' general manager, at Boston's surprising seventh-game victory over the Los Angeles Lakers in 1969. It was a specially sweet championship for him, since the Lakers with their great center, Wilt Chamberlain, were not only a heavy favorite to win the Series, but the deciding seventh game was being played in the Spectrum, their home court. As it happened, Wilt Chamberlain sat out the last few minutes, and a thick, colorful cluster of balloons, planned to be set loose onto the court at the instant of the final buzzer, remained fixed to the ceiling high above. Just as Auerbach was lighting his large victory cigar—it was a well-known gesture of triumph he had affected over the years—a woman suddenly appeared in the aisle in front of us and darting an aerosol can in his face she squirted him (and the cigar, which went out) with a large dollopy portion of shaving cream. It seems funny in retrospect—a pie-in-the-face routine—especially with the homey, familiar face of Auerbach as the target, but it was not at all funny at the time: behind the can the woman's face was contorted with rage; she yelled something manic and indistinguishable in the uproar. It terrified Auerbach. He mopped at the shaving cream with his coat sleeve. His face emerged mottled and upset.

Timothy: "Now let's just see. After the battle of Kossovo in 1389, the Sultan Morad I absolutely annihilated the Serbs—Blackbirds' Field, you'll recall—and he was rejoicing in this enormous victory of Turkish might, just like your friend Auerbach, when suddenly a Serb named Milos Kobil cut him down at the moment of victory. The assassin, of course, became a hero, and still is, to patriotic Serbs, though they purposely mispronounce his name. Kobil means 'son-of-a-brood-mare.' It would hardly do to have a national hero with a name like that. So it's pronounced *Obilich.* It's better."

"Perhaps," I said. "It's difficult for me to tell."

"Not if you were a Serb," Timothy said. "Then, of course, to follow up, we have the tragic, if romantic and celebrated case of Pheidippides, who ran from the battle of Marathon to Athens to bring news of the victory over the Persians in 490 B.C. Staggering into the marketplace, he cried out, 'Rejoice, we conquer!' and then collapsed and died."

I said, "Well, yes, but I wouldn't want to suggest that the fit conclusion to a day's work for an athlete is what happened to Pheidippides and the Serb."

In fact (I went on to say) what we envied so much about the athlete was that the end of a day's competition was always tempered for the length of his competitive life by the knowledge that the keenness of putting his skills on the line would be

49

experienced—presumably to his enjoyment—very soon again. Not only did the athlete possess immense physical skills, but he had the opportunity to exercise them in highly ritualized dramatic settings, often every day! Could there be anything better in life than waking up in the morning, and looking to see how many hours one had to dawdle away, feeling the pressures mount, before going out to the ball park for a game?

Even when their careers are over, there remains the richness of recall. I once asked a number of athletes if they would supply a description that might be representative of some special moment in their careers—not an actual photograph, but a verbal description of some instant caught in memory, like a fly in amber (a phenomenon I have heard of many times and find a splendid image, but have not actually witnessed), which they could offer for a book of this sort. It would not be inappropriate to match Mr. Leifer's photographs with a few examples of what athletes carry around in their heads, some frozen moment, like a snapshot in a wallet, would it? And then, Timothy, we can go to the Russian Tea Room and you can tell me what Oliver Cromwell wrote on Henry Marten's face, and what Cromwell got written on his. That little scene has settled in my head like a fly in er. . . and I am not at ease. Now let us have our monographs.

Timothy: "Who are these people?"

They are representative. Many friends. That would be enough.

Ken Dryden, hockey goalie: *"It was an instant—seemingly quite obscure—in a college game between Cornell and Boston University. I suddenly realized that I was using my leg pads to stop the puck. Before that game I had always done what was natural for me: to spear at the puck with my gloved hand like catching a baseball. When I used the pads that day I knew I had graduated. I was suddenly on a different plateau with all its possibilities. And I realized for the first time, or perhaps I should say that the* suspicion *crossed my mind, that I could be very, very good."*

John Havlicek, basketball player: When he played at Ohio State before coming to the Boston Celtics, Havlicek was what was known then as a "garbage man"—a player whose chief function was to shovel the ball to the higher scorers. He thought he would continue to do that with the Boston team, which had, after all, a number of superb gunners—Bailey Howell, Satch Sanders, Sam Jones, K.C. Jones, among others. Havlicek was so resigned to this activity that when Red Auerbach, the coach, called him into his office and told him he wanted him to *shoot*, there was nothing about that instant Havlicek would ever forget: he remembers the weather outside the window, what suit Auerbach was wearing, the smell of his cigar, the arrangement of the letter-openers (which Auerbach collects) on his desk, and, of course, the exact wording of what Auerbach told him: "You can't let them insult you. *Shoot!*" Havlicek was so startled that he asked Auerbach to repeat what he had said. He wanted to be sure.

Eddie Arcaro, jockey: *"I think back more often than I like—I don't seem to be able to stop doing it—on the Kentucky Derby in 1947 when Jet Pilot beat the horse I was riding, Phalanx, just at the wire. We should have won. Phalanx was a better horse. In fact, when I think back and run the race in my mind we* do *win. Phalanx was a clumsy runner, not a horse that you can guide through a crowded field like Citation, who could be slowed down and speeded up, like throwing a racing car in and out of gear. Phalanx was a kind of plodder—that is to say you could push him to run faster and faster but there was no craft to him: it was like getting a boulder rolling down a hill. The trouble with that is that with a horse you can't go through other horses. So in that '47 Derby the horses fanned out coming down the stretch, rather than staying bunched, and we had too far to go around. Jet Pilot had one jump on us and if the finish line had been ten yards down the track we would have won. As it is, in those flashbacks of mine he does win. Of course, that doesn't show up in the charts."*

Jim Brown, football player: *"It was an exhibition game in Canton, Ohio. I took a hand-off on a trap play, and I broke through the line into the open. Two of their defensive people converged on me, coming in at angles that made it very difficult for me, but I managed to move so that they came together* here *when I was* there. *Paul Brown, who was the head coach, said, 'You can take a rest, man, you're my fullback.'"*

Henry Aaron, baseball player: *"Of course, I remember my 715th home run which broke Babe Ruth's record, but not as much as you'd think. I remember mainly the relief when I hit it...like a stove had been lifted from my back. I don't remember the Dodgers congratulating me on the base path—that was the team we played that night—or the two kids who ran onto the field to shake my hand. What I particularly remember is that my mother appeared at home plate. They rushed her out there as soon as the ball was hit. I suppose anyone would remember that...his mother suddenly appearing at home plate!*

"But the true instant for me, like a photograph, was home run number 109, which I hit in the 11th inning of a 2-2 tie which defeated the Cardinals and gave us—the Milwaukee Braves—the pennant in 1957. I can remember everything about running the bases—even what I was thinking!...which was about Bobby Thomson's miracle home run, which I had heard on the radio down in Mobile, Alabama, when I was a kid. As I ran the bases I thought, my, now I've got one for myself!"

Ken Venturi, golfer: His instant was the most dramatic golf hole of his life—the 18th at the Congressional on the day in 1964, with the temperature in the 100s, when he won the U.S. Open. In that great heat he overcame years of vicissitude and personal problems, including everything from drinking difficulties to a circulation ailment in his hand. He'd had terrible back spasms; he couldn't lift his arms over his head. In 1963 he had only won 3,800 dollars. On the day of his Open victory the doctors advised him to stop, that in the heat he would go into convulsions if he continued. On the 18th, barely able to put one foot in front of the other, he dropped his putter after his final putt, the realization flooding in on him, and he cried out, "My God, I've won the Open!" But the only thing he remembers about that climactic moment is that two marshalls, who were supposed to be controlling the crowd, fell into a fight, pushing at each other and shouting, for a view to see him sink that final putt.

Jim Whitaker, mountain climber: "Up on Everest it's 35 degrees below zero. It takes as much as three hours to go 300 yards, averaging ten breaths for every step taken. The mind moves almost as slowly at that extreme altitude. The smallest problems become extremely difficult. One of them facing me during the ascent—and it wasn't all that minor either—was that like an idiot I hadn't gone to the bathroom at the camp before setting out. The situation became critical. My mind was just barely ticking over as I tried to focus on the consequences of going ahead—the major one being that frostbite seizes the bare skin within sixty seconds, even something as fatty as a rear end. Well, rather than doing it with my trousers on, I took the risk, and got away with it. A quickie. Those few seconds stay in my mind."

Tom Matte, football player: "I miss the training camp. When it was on, it meant total security, where one was totally oblivious of the outside world—a sort of Shangri-La completely apart from reality, where there wasn't a worry in the world, where everything was taken care of for you, and you were with people who were going to stand by you...the camaraderie...the friendships...it's the one atmosphere that I remember above all else."

A Bullfighter: I don't remember his name. But I remember his telling me about the bulls and how their looks were enhanced by a long, flowing tail when they came out of the toril into the arena. Indeed, if a bull on the breeding ranch happened to lose his tail on a fence, which occasionally happened, the ranchers patched on another just before the bull was shipped to where he was to appear in the plaza. The reputation of the ganadero had to be upheld. Once, the bullfighter had been bumped hard by a bull and down he went. His quadrilla rushed out to flop capes to distract the bull and one of them reached for the bull's tail to turn him off the matador. That was the moment the bullfighter remembered, being down, looking up beyond the bull's head, the horns straddling him, rasping against the sand, and seeing the tail come away in the peon's hand, and remembering the look of the man's face as he stared down at what had been attached to 500 kilos of bull and now was as limp and insignificant as a fly whisk.

Frank Shorter, marathon runner: "One of the pleasures of distance running is that it is nicely ambiguous...non-structured...and you're not forced to explain it. But there are two feelings I am conscious of, and they are very related. The first, crossing the *finish line to win the marathon at Munich—everything, symbolically and realistically, came into place. Up until then I hadn't realized there was a finish line. And then second, is the feeling you get when you train in the mountains with those great distances to look over, and nearer at hand everything's so clear and sharp—the beaver in the ponds—so that it's almost unreal. And there's such a feeling of liking being there and what you're doing that sometimes I think I race just so I can train and enjoy that feeling. And then sometimes I think I train so I can cross the finish line and enjoy that feeling. It's nicely related."*

Roy Williams, ex-Detroit Lion football player: *"I haven't watched a Super Bowl game, or in fact any professional football since I left the game. I've cut football out of my life. It sounds like heresy, doesn't it? A lot of people don't understand it, so I don't tell them. The reason for not going to games is that I had always realized football was a business, so from the beginning it didn't make any more sense for me to watch football than it would for a writer to sit in front of a television set and watch other writers write. You'd get bored. But you must understand that while my value system has changed, I would never deprecate football. It provided a foundation to learn the fundamentals—confidence, tenacity, competitiveness, the price of excellence—those are all in football and you absorb them without being crucially destroyed, which might happen if you had to learn these things, and make the mistakes, outside in the commercial world. If I were to watch football, it would be to see it through the eyes of my children. There are social possibilities. Still, I find talk about football boring. I'd much rather talk about things I don't know much about, or what I'm working on now—economics, or political history. When I think back I see myself standing in the middle of a huge stadium at kickoff time—you feel alone out there, I would suppose like a Roman gladiator once felt—and hearing that strange hissing roar out of the great crowd as the referee brings down his arm. I don't know how we've transcended from those Roman times. There's almost as much blood, though at least not as many people are dying."*

Jackie Stewart, racing driver: *"When I look at racing, I can hardly believe I had anything to do with it. It looks so truly extraordinary; my God, those drivers are supermen. Of course, I had never seen it from the perspective of a witness. So when I went to Monte Carlo and saw my first race after retiring I found myself astonished at the speeds in those narrow streets, the fractions of inches at the corners. I could hardly imagine the talent involved. Of course, the exhilaration of doing it myself still comes back. When I reached a certain stage of my development as a race car driver I could fully appreciate the flavor of it. It's not unlike the progression one goes through to appreciate good food and wine: it's not automatic; one advances, and suddenly there's an awareness of what the flavors truly express. The phenomenon occurs in racing, and the memory of that awareness still lingers; it comes back with a nice combination of nostalgia and wonder: 'Oh damn, that was good!' "*

Timothy: "You must have one yourself."

Someone asked me a while ago if I had any moment of this sort to recall. I finally replied that for some time I had kept thinking of a story that Mark "The Bird" Fidrych had told me. We were driving in a heavy snowstorm toward Detroit's Metropolitan Airport. The cassette player in his car was featuring a musical group called the Fog Heads, who provided a loud and appropriate accompaniment to the buffeting of the weather outside. Fidrych was saying that he had picked up a hitchhiker in the rain one afternoon. The man had gotten in the car, thanked him, and almost immediately announced that he was in financial trouble—he had been laid off at some automotive plant—and he asked Fidrych if he could borrow five dollars. The Bird grumbled, but he reached in his jeans and pulled out a five dollar bill, whereupon the hitchhiker remarked about how *long* he had been laid off, and while his benefactor was about it, wouldn't *fifteen* dollars be a little better than five?

The Bird balked at this; he said he wasn't in the habit of lending money to hitchhikers in the first place.

"Did he recognize you?" I asked.

Fidrych shook his head. "No, he didn't"—which surprised me since I would have assumed that anyone in the Detroit area would have known the long boyish face under the strange mop of ringlet hair, the beanpole frame in the blue jeans, his knees cramped up under the steering wheel.

"But then I told him I worked for a living," The Bird said, "I told him what I did."

"How did you describe it to him?" I found myself asking him.

He looked over. "Well, I told him I played ball. I was a pitcher."

That was the phrase I remembered, envying the almost exquisite pleasure it must be to inform a stranger—even one that had touched you for five or even fifteen dollars—that what one did was to play ball, *a pitcher,* what's more.

Robert Frost once admitted to exactly this: that riding in the rear corner of a Boston & Maine Railroad car he had always hoped that the people chatting together down the aisle, glancing over and probably speculating about him, were speaking of him as looking like an ex-ballplayer, very likely a pitcher, and maybe long past his prime, but *certainly* he had been at one time...

I guess we all knew what he was talking about. What a gentle and foolish people we were.

THE PHOTOGRAPHS

11. USC football
    team huddle,
    Los Angeles,
    November, 1972

12. Astrodome,
    Houston, Texas,
    May, 1966

13. Tom Yawkey,
    owner of the Boston Red Sox,
    Fenway Park, Boston,
    July, 1975

Overleaf:

14. Mark Spitz,
    Beverly Hills, California,
    September, 1976

15. Pole vault,
Russian–American
Track Meet,
Minsk, USSR,
July, 1973

16. Hot Dog skiing,
 Vail, Colorado,
 September, 1972

17. Nadia Comaneci,
 All-around gold medalist,
 Olympic Games,
 Montreal, Canada,
 August, 1976

18. Nadia Comaneci,
    Olympic Games,
    Montreal, Canada,
    August, 1976

19. Bob Brown,
    Oakland Raiders,
    Oakland, California,
    November, 1971

20. Fran Tarkenton,
    Minnesota Vikings quarterback,
    October, 1975

21. Sonny Liston,
    Las Vegas, Nevada,
    May, 1967

22. Vassily Alexeev,
world record lift,
European Championships,
Szombathely, Hungary,
June, 1970

Following pages:

23. English relay team,
Olympic Games,
Mexico City,
October, 1968

24. Steeplechase runners,
Olympic trials,
Eugene, Oregon,
June, 1972

25. Dick Butkus,
    Chicago Bears linebacker,
    October, 1969

26. Joe Namath,
    New York Jets quarterback,
    Shea Stadium,
    November, 1974

27. Burt Reynolds,
     filming of *The Longest Yard,*
     Georgia State Penitentiary,
     Reidsville, Georgia,
     December, 1973

28. Muhammad Ali,
    training camp,
    Miami, Florida,
    September, 1970

29. Secretariat winning
    the Kentucky Derby,
    Churchill Downs, Kentucky,
    May, 1973

30. Start of the marathon,
    Olympic Games,
    Munich, Germany,
    August, 1972

31. Frank Shorter
winning the marathon,
Olympic Games,
Munich, Germany,
August, 1972

33. Reggie Jackson,
    Yankee Stadium,
    New York,
    April, 1977

32. Bjorn Borg,
    Wimbledon final,
    London,
    June, 1976

34. World Series action,
    Yankees versus Dodgers,
    Yankee Stadium,
    October, 1977

35. Willie Mays,
    Shea Stadium,
    New York,
    May, 1972

36. Sam Huff, New York Giants linebacker,
    Yankee Stadium, November, 1962

37. FA Cup Final, Wembley Stadium,
    London, England, May, 1971

Overleaf:

38. Boys playing soccer, Dix Hills,
    New York, September, 1977

41. Jack Nicklaus,
Augusta, Georgia,
April, 1972

Preceding page:
39. Masters Golf Tournament, Augusta, Georgia, April, 1975

Opposite:
40. Tom Watson, Hawaiian Open, February, 1977

42. America's Cup Race,
    Newport, Rhode Island,
    September, 1967

43. Iceboating, Green Lake, Wisconsin, January, 1964

Overleaf:

44. Iceboat race,
    Lake Geneva, Wisconsin,
    January, 1964

45. Franz Klammer,
    Winter Olympics,
    Innsbruck, Austria,
    February, 1976

46. Top of the 70–meter
    ski jump,
    Sapporo, Japan,
    January, 1971

48. Micki King diving, Tampa, Florida, June, 1971

47. Skiing moguls,
      Sun Valley, Idaho,
      March, 1974

Overleaf:
49. Surfing, Hawaii,
      December, 1967

52. The International,
    Roosevelt Raceway,
    New York, July, 1968

53. College basketball,
    Greensboro, North Carolina,
    March, 1976

54. Garfield Heard
    at the basket,
    Buffalo Braves versus
    Washington Bullets,
    Buffalo, New York,
    April, 1975

55. Bob Seagren,
    world record vault,
    AAU National Championships,
    Albuquerque, New Mexico,
    March, 1966

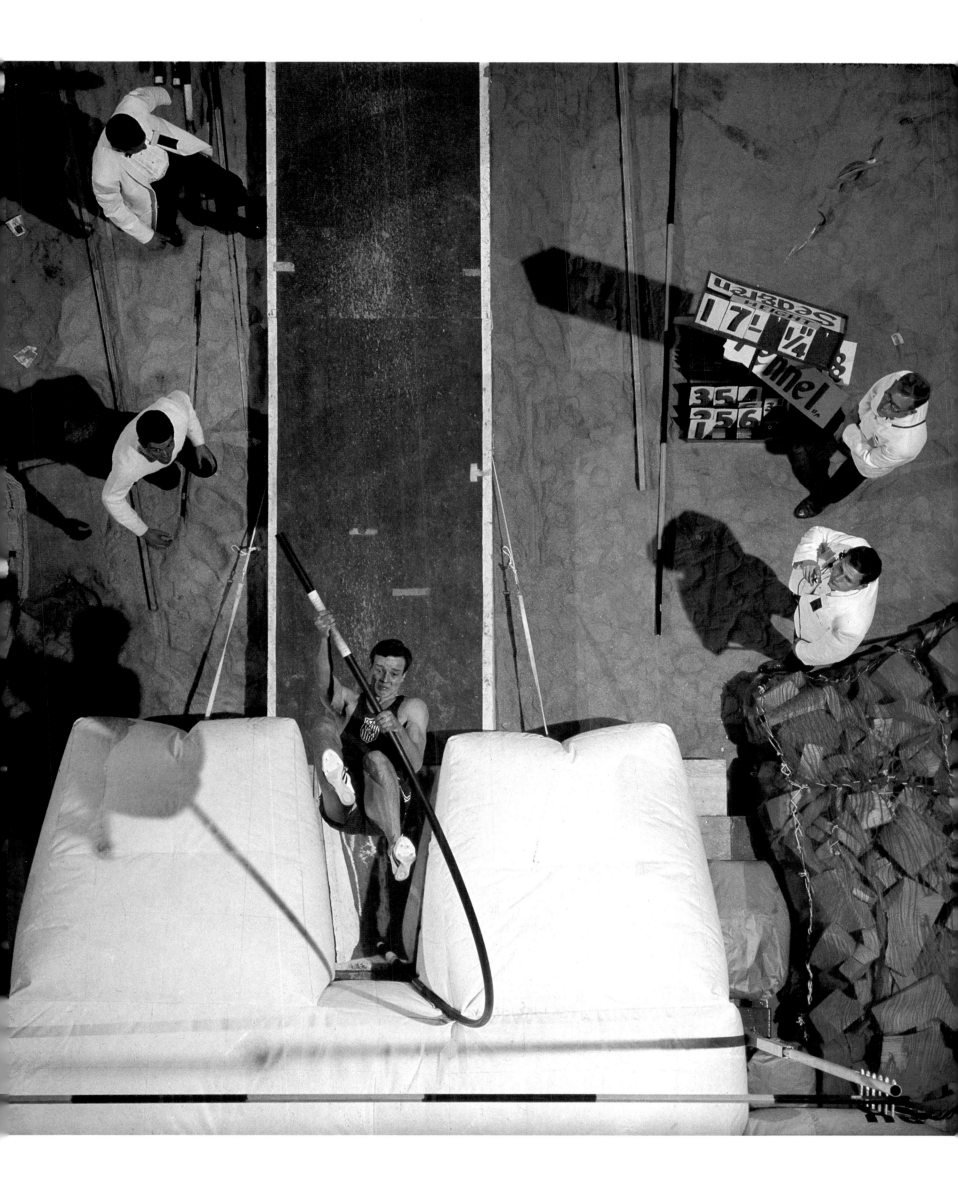

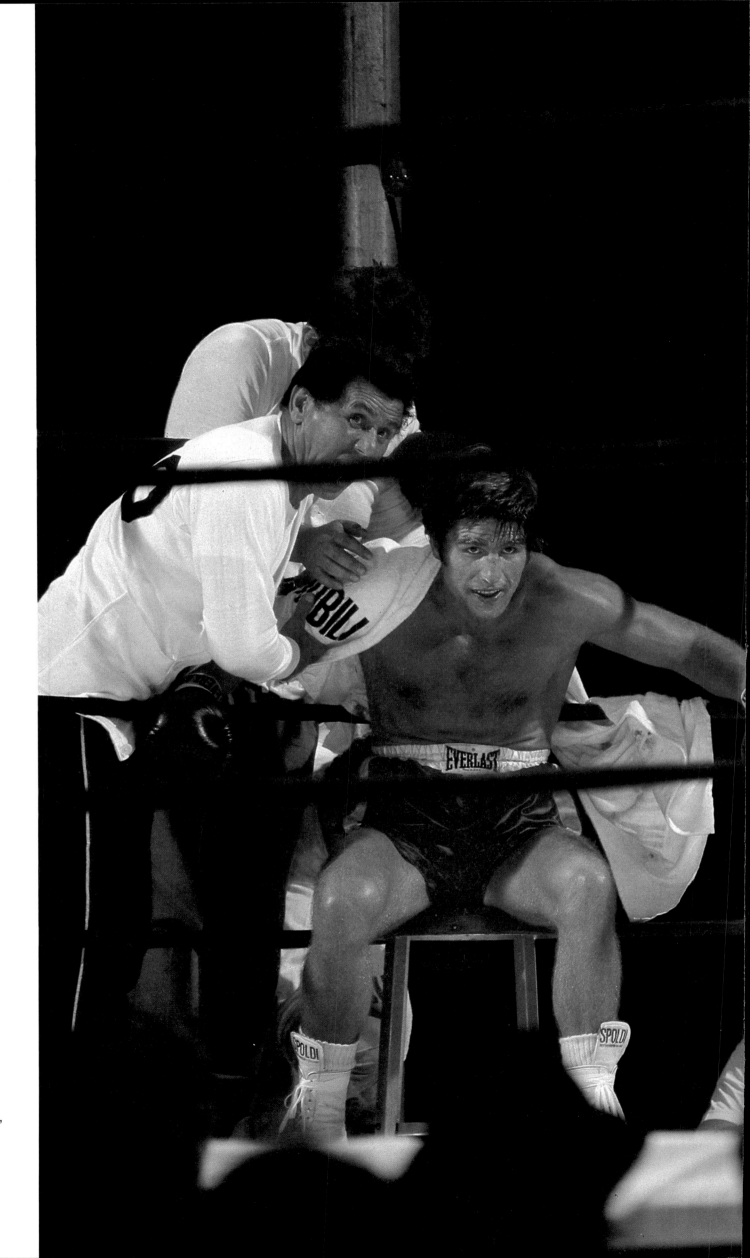

56. Nino Benvenuti–
    Emile Griffith fight,
    Shea Stadium, New York,
    September, 1967

Overleaf:

57. Muhammad Ali–
    Bob Foster fight,
    Lake Tahoe, Nevada,
    November, 1972

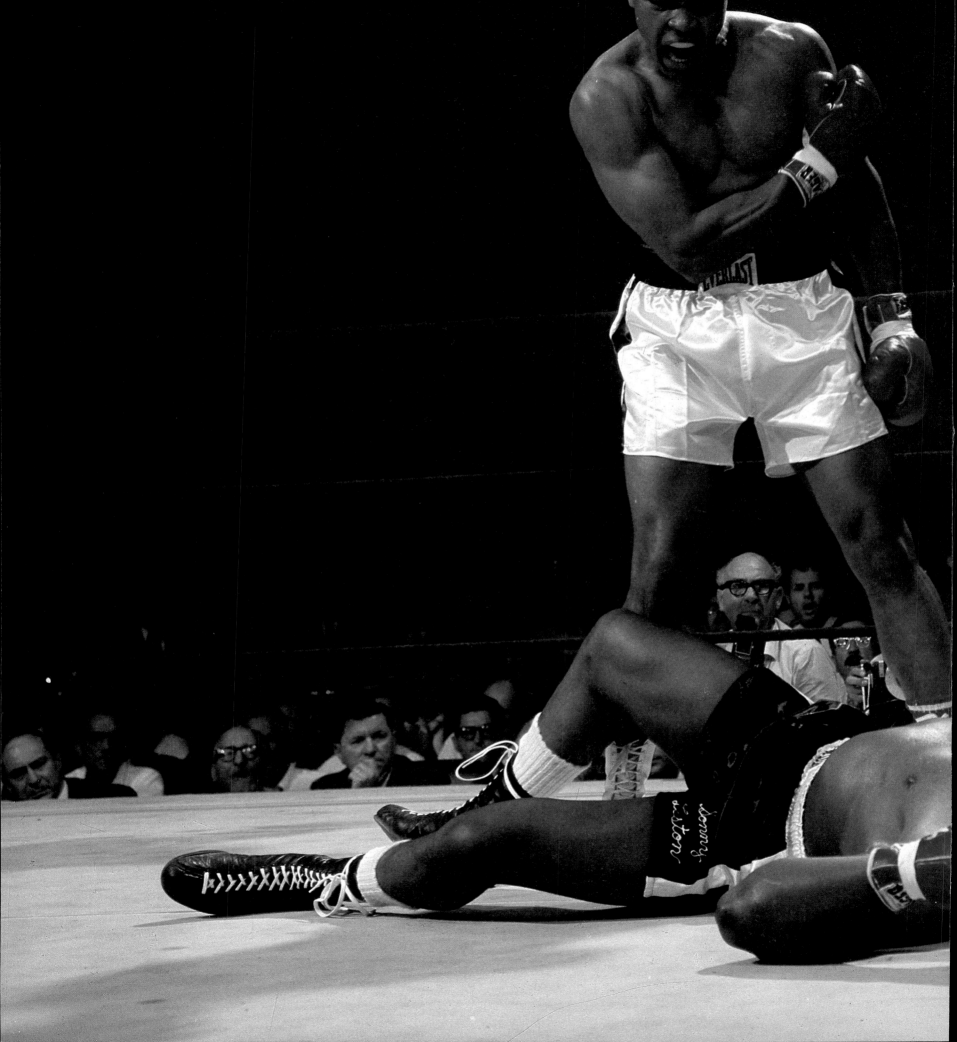

58. Muhammad Ali
(Cassius Clay)
KO's Sonny Liston,
Lewiston, Maine,
May, 1965

59. Joe Frazier after losing
    to Muhammad Ali
    in the 14th round,
    Manila, Philippines,
    October, 1975

60. Don King,
    boxing promoter,
    New York, July, 1975

61. President Gerald Ford
    skiing at Vail, Colorado,
    December, 1975

62. Vince Lombardi,
    Green Bay Packer coach,
    after winning
    the Super Bowl,
    Miami, Florida,
    January, 1968

63. Floyd Patterson–Jerry Quarry fight,
    Los Angeles, October, 1967

64. Willie Shoemaker
    riding Northern Dancer
    in the Florida Derby,
    Hallandale, Florida, April, 1964

65. Touchdown catch, Buffalo Bills versus New York Jets, Shea Stadium, New York, November, 1974

66. USC versus Michigan, Rose Bowl, Pasadena, California, January, 1977

67. Buffalo Bills versus New York Jets, Shea Stadium, November, 1974

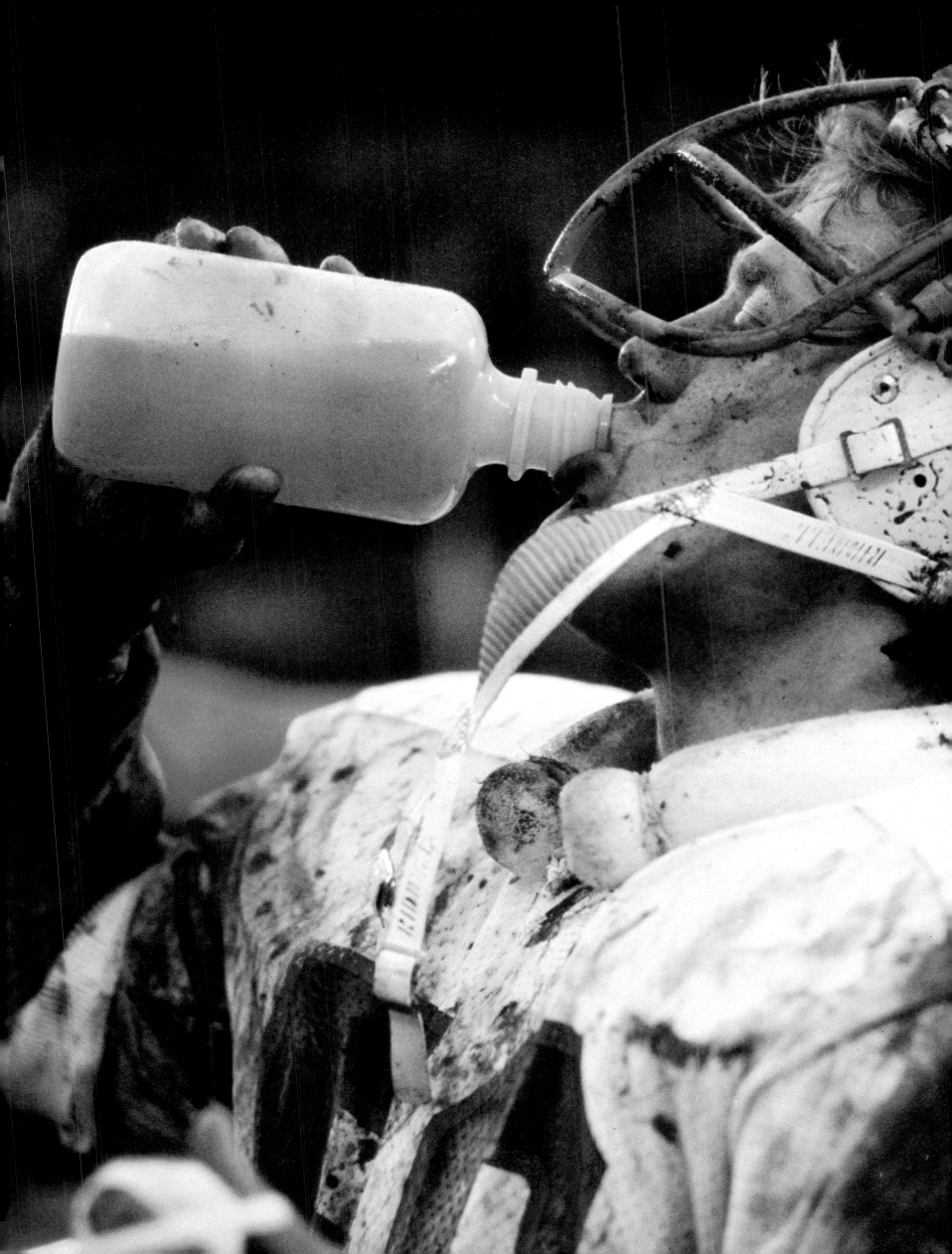

Preceding page:
68. Boston Bruins versus St. Louis Blues,
    Boston Garden, April, 1972

70. Jack Nicklaus
    at Augusta National Golf Course,
    Augusta, Georgia,
    April, 1977

69. Bobby Hull
    of the Chicago Black Hawks,
    Chicago, February, 1967

71. George McGinnis
    of the Philadelphia '76ers,
    Philadelphia,
    March, 1977

72. NBA Playoffs,
    Braves versus Bullets,
    Baltimore,
    April, 1975

73. Jockey Steve Cauthen,
    Aqueduct Race Track,
    New York, February, 1977

74. Sugar Ray Robinson,
    Honolulu, Hawaii,
    August, 1965

75. University of Oregon
    cheerleader,
    Eugene, Oregon,
    February, 1975

76. Casey Stengel,
    Polo Grounds,
    New York,
    June, 1962

77. Skier, Aspen,
    Colorado,
    December, 1970

Overleaf:

78. Bobsledding,
    Winter Olympics,
    Innsbruck, Austria,
    February, 1976

79. French Grand Prix, Circuit Paul Ricard, France, June, 1973

S'AFET

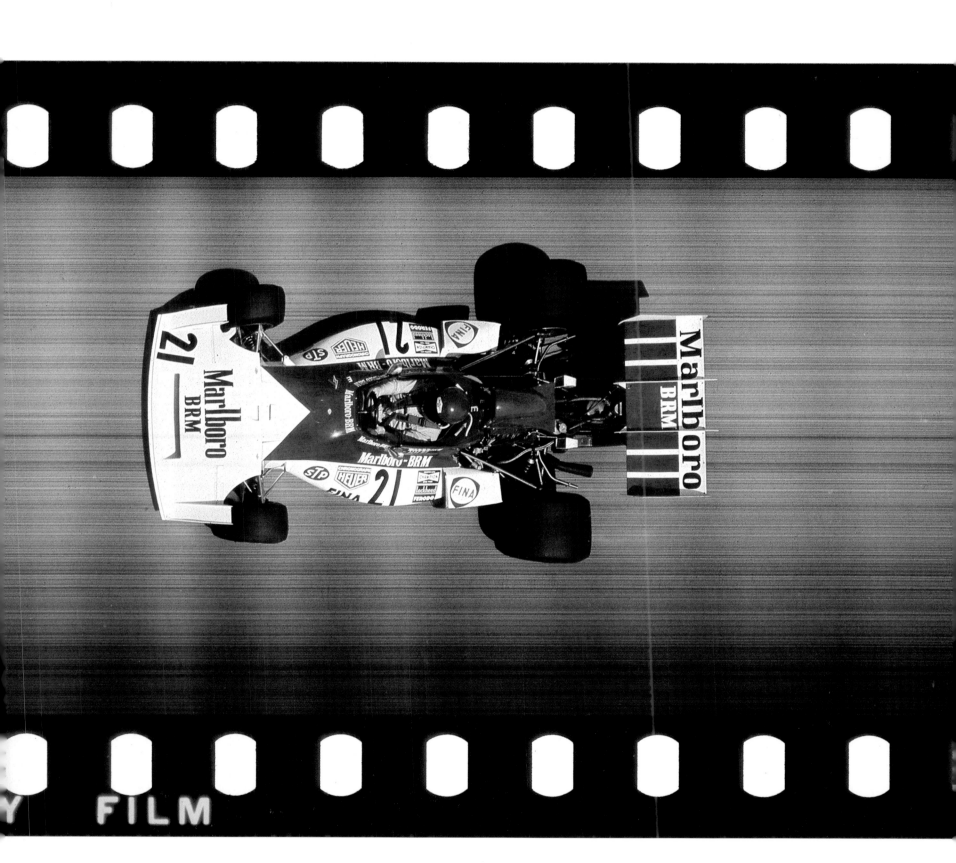

86. Race driver
     Jackie Stewart at
     the French Grand Prix,
     June, 1973

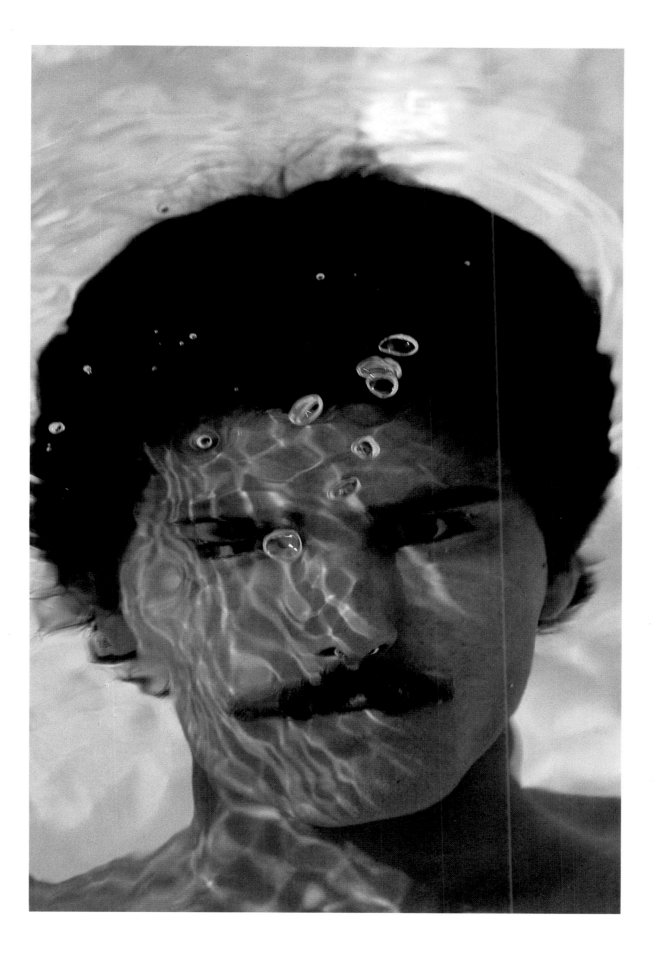

87. Olympic swimmer
Mark Spitz,
Beverly Hills, California,
May, 1976

88. Slalom,
    Winter Olympics,
    Innsbruck, Austria,
    February, 1976

Overleaf:

89. Monoskiing,
    Sun Valley, Idaho,
    March, 1974

90. Chuck Wepner before his title fight with Muhammad Ali,
    Catskills training camp, February, 1975

91. Ken Norton before his title fight with Muhammad Ali,
    New York, August, 1976

99. Muhammad Ali (Cassius Clay)
knocks out Cleveland Williams
at 1:08 of the third round,
Astrodome, Houston, Texas,
November, 1966

NOTES ON THE PHOTOGRAPHS

Technical Note:
Neil Leifer customarily uses 35mm Nikon cameras with motor drive and Nikkor lenses. In the following captions, unless otherwise indicated, all the equipment is by Nikon. Kodak films were used throughout and are specified.

All the captions were written by Neil Leifer.

100. Dorothy Hamill,
    gold medalist figure skater,
    Winter Olympics,
    Innsbruck, Austria,
    February, 1976

1. Good sports photography is usually the result of careful planning, good luck and good execution. This picture is testimonial to none of the three. My intention was to shoot the opening tap of the Boston Celtics–Chicago Bulls basketball game with a close-up of Nate Thurmond and Dave Cowens reaching up toward the ceiling for the ball. I positioned myself 80 feet above the floor on the Boston Garden catwalk and waited for the jump. When Thurmond and Cowens came out, I clicked off a few just to check the focus as they were shaking hands and then shot the opening tap. When I got the roll of film back, the picture of the opening tap was wonderful but not nearly as good, I thought, as this picture of the handshake.

   300mm f2.8 lens, high speed Ektachrome daylight film pushed to 400 ASA.

2. Possibly the most exciting moment at any Olympic Games is the arrival of the Olympic flame in the stadium at the opening ceremonies. This picture was taken during the 1976 Winter Olympic Games in Innsbruck and shows the torchbearer midway up the runway on his way to light the flame. I deliberately chose a long lens to eliminate all the extraneous matter in the picture and close in on the torchbearer and the honor guard that surrounded the runway to the flame.

   200mm f4 lens, EPD Ektachrome 200 ASA.

3. The 1974 Kentucky Derby was extra special for two reasons. First, it was the 100th running of the classic and secondly, it contained the largest field in Derby history. This picture was taken with a camera mounted just above the stall of the first horse in order to see the entire field at the start and also capture both the crowd and famed spires of Churchill Downs. The hand in the lower right-hand corner belongs to an assistant trainer who makes sure the horses break cleanly from the gate.

   15mm f5.6 lens, high speed Ektachrome daylight film.

4. Chris Evert's serve provides a wonderful opportunity to study perfection. This picture shows grace and concentration at its best: it was taken while Chrissie was winning a Virginia Slims tournament in Madison Square Garden.

   300mm f2.8 lens, Kodak EPT 160 ASA film pushed to 400 ASA.

170

5. Grace, power and concentration are manifest in this picture of Juan Marichal pitching. Marichal, who pitched for many years for the San Francisco Giants, was known for his high kick. This picture was made during spring training.

   600mm f5.6 lens, Kodachrome film.

6. After two days of careful planning, I decided that the best way to photograph the start of the 1975 Boston Marathon was to rent a cherry picker truck crane and position myself midway over the road about 200 yards down from the starting line. I took time to check out the scene with each of the lenses I had with me, and after selecting the lens I most wanted to use, all that was left to do was wait. Except for the spectators lining the route, the street looked just as quiet as it always does. Finally, the gun went off and seconds later, this mass of humanity came running right beneath the camera. It left me with goose bumps and I'll never forget it as one of the most exciting sights I've ever seen in sport. Half an hour after this picture was taken, just as I was ready to leave the scene, I looked down the street and once again it was just a small, quiet New England country street that would stay that way until the 1976 Boston Marathon was run.

   24mm lens, Kodachrome.

7. There's a wonderful contrast between this picture and the one at the start of the Boston Marathon. This photograph was taken in a small French town called Brest and it shows the start of the Tour de France bike race moments after the racers had turned the first corner with a whole day's pedaling still ahead. In this picture I used a long lens to squeeze in the group of bike riders as well as show the spectators and buildings that line both sides of the street.

   200mm f4 lens, Kodachrome.

8. Ask anybody who has really been around sports and they'll tell you that far and away the most exciting, the most spectacular and most beautiful event in the world is the Monaco Grand Prix. This photograph was taken moments after the start at what is known as the Casino Turn and shows the cars strung out like toys just in front of the Hotel de Paris with the Grand Casino of Monte Carlo in the background. It is a sight that anyone who has ever seen will never forget; in my opinion, it ranks among the most exciting moments in all of sport. The picture was taken from a television tower.

   24mm lens, Kodachrome film.

9. The idea for this picture was simple enough. The New York marathon begins on the Verrazano-Narrows Bridge and weaves its way for 26 miles through all five boroughs of New York. I felt that the most exciting moment would take place when all 5,000 runners try to squeeze their way down one lane of the bridge. I rented a helicopter and my plan was simply to position myself over the Brooklyn end of the bridge and wait for the runners to go beneath the helicopter. What I hadn't counted on was that every other photographer in town had also rented a helicopter. So the trick here was really to get a helicopter pilot who had the guts to hang in there while helicopters hovered above and below and to each side of us. This picture is really a testimonial to the pilot who flew the helicopter, rather than to me.

   50mm lens, Ektachrome EPD film.

10. To photograph the opening face-off of a Ranger hockey game, I suspended a fish-eye camera 50 feet above the center circle at the old Madison Square Garden. We then lit all seats in the Garden with eight banks of strobe lights and wired them to the camera so that they could be fired remotely from my seat. Once all this was done, the picture was a snap to shoot. All I did was wait for the referee to drop the puck; I pressed the button, the lights went off, the camera clicked and I kept my fingers crossed until the film came back from the lab.

    Fish-eye lens, Kodachrome.

11. A good photographer is supposed to learn by his mistakes. This picture, which shows the 1972 National Championship USC team from inside their huddle, is the result of one of my biggest mistakes. I had first tried this picture, two or three years earlier, with an Arkansas football team. After carefully arranging with the Coach to have the offensive starting team pose for me, I set about readying myself for the photograph. The camera was placed on its back in a special rig with two small strobe lights flanking it to light up the inside of the huddle. Suddenly, the Arkansas football team appeared. I quickly gave them my best Knute Rockne speech and told them how important this picture was to me and how much they would enjoy seeing it on the cover of *Sports Illustrated*. I then got back 30 or 40 feet to fire the camera remotely and take the picture. When I had finished shooting enough frames to satisfy

12

13

14

15

16

17

18

19

20

21

22

myself, I thanked each of the players and headed back with the film.

The pictures were beautiful and it never dawned on me that anything might be wrong until my picture editor came out of the meeting in which the week's cover photograph would be chosen. When the pictures had been shown to the managing editor, somebody said that it looked a bit funny because there were one too many halfbacks in the huddle—at which point somebody decided to count the players. Sure enough, instead of 11, the Arkansas coach had sent me 12. Needless to say, that photograph never ran. But this one was certainly the result of the previous failure. And before I permitted myself to shoot the first frame I counted each player four times.

Fish-eye lens, Kodachrome.

12. Some pictures are very, very easy to take if you can only get to the right place. Before the Houston Astrodome was opened in the mid-1960s, a picture like this could only have been taken from a helicopter or blimp. The Astrodome, however, has a gondola 208 feet over the center of the arena and for those willing to brave their way up, it's a beautiful place to watch a ball game. You can't buy a hot dog, you can't buy a beer, but you surely have the best seat in the house.

50mm lens, high speed Ektachrome daylight film.

13. The late Tom Yawkey was Mr. Baseball to many generations of Boston Red Sox fans. Doing a story at Fenway Park on baseball's new boom, I couldn't help noticing Yawkey sitting in the owner's box about 75 feet away and to my right. Reflected in his sunglasses was the Fenway Park he loved so much—and for so long.

400mm f5.6 lens, high speed Ektachrome daylight film.

14. Certainly one of the greatest single achievements in sport in our lifetimes will be the seven gold medals that Mark Spitz won at the 1972 Olympic Games in Munich. This picture, taken at a backyard pool in Beverly Hills, California, almost four years after his Munich triumph, shows that Mark's condition was still the same as it had been in Munich. I took this picture by walking up and down the pool parallel to him as he swam.

200mm f4 lens, Kodachrome film.

172

15. I call this the ultimate "Big Brother is watching you" picture. I took it in Minsk in the Soviet Union during the Russian–American Track Meet in 1973. The stadium in Minsk looked like most other stadiums I'd seen before, except for the imposing portrait of Lenin which looked down upon the field from just behind the pole vault pit. During the pole vault competition, I waited beneath the bar for a vaulter to go over the top and shot this picture as an American vaulter cleared the top—despite the menacing look of Lenin.

    24mm lens, Ektachrome 64 ASA film.

16. One look at this photograph and it's easy to see why hot dog skiing—a relatively new sport—is already a favorite among photographers. All you need do is position yourself beneath one of the jumps and the view is spectacular enough to make great pictures no matter what the camera, lens or conditions. I took this picture during a competition in Vail, Colorado, in 1972.

    24mm lens, Kodachrome film.

17. The star of the 1976 Summer Olympic Games in Montreal was Nadia Comaneci. Gymnastics always produces beautiful pictures, and Nadia was not about to let down any photographer who had the opportunity to cover the competition in Montreal. While most spectators look to the floor exercise as the most exciting event of the women's gymnastics, photographers generally find that the best pictures are taken on the balance beam. This picture was taken during Nadia's gold medal–winning performance on the balance beam.

    85mm lens, daylight EPD 200 speed film, pushed to 800 ASA.

18. Here is another photograph of Nadia Comaneci performing on the balance beam during the 1976 Montreal Olympic Games. One of the things you can do with still photography of an event like gymnastics is to freeze perfection and I think this picture does just that. It catches a moment when Nadia is looking absolutely serene while performing a difficult maneuver on the balance beam.

    135mm f2 lens, Ektachrome.

19. While most football fans can name the quarterbacks and running backs and important linebackers in football, very few know the offensive linemen. Bob Brown, who played with the Oakland Raiders, is one of the most charismatic players I've ever photographed. He made good pictures in the game or on the bench.

    85mm f1.8 lens, a Nikkormat EL camera, and high speed Ektachrome type B film.

20. Minnesota Viking quarterback Fran Tarkenton helped me take this picture by first drawing a series of Minnesota's offensive plays on the blackboard. I photographed the plays on a number of rolls of film and then set up the portrait of Fran Tarkenton against the black background and ran the same film that already had the plays on it through the camera. The resulting picture, I think, gives you the feeling of Fran Tarkenton studying his playbook and gives you a little bit of the idea of the complexity of professional football.

    Hasselblad camera with a 150mm lens, Ektachrome film and strobe lighting.

21. When I took this picture of Sonny Liston in the casino at Caesar's Palace in Las Vegas he was already three years removed from his World Heavyweight Championship title but was still gambling on a comeback. Sonny was a very easy subject to photograph. I wanted a stern, hard, cold look and that's the only look Sonny knew how to give. I sat him down at the head of the blackjack table, and also at the roulette table and said, "Sonny, sit" and Sonny sat. "Sonny, stare" and Sonny stared and the picture session went very, very easily.

    Hasselblad camera with a 150mm lens, strobe lighting using colored gels.

22. Following his gold medal wins in the Montreal and the Munich Olympic Games, Vassily Alexeev became a household word to most sports fans. This picture, however, was shot in June of 1970 when he was relatively unknown in the West. It was taken in a small town in Hungary called Szombathely, where the European Weight Lifting Championships were being held. They had never seen a photographer from the West in this town, and didn't quite know how to handle the situation. I set up my strobes to light the weight lifting area and picked the position I wanted to shoot from. It turned out that a television camera was already positioned there. Well, before I knew it, there was a small conference

173

and rather than move me, they moved the television camera—something that has never happened before and I'm sure will never happen again.

While working, I was standing in a well at about floor level just in front of where the weight lifter was and about two lifts before I took this picture, one of the lifters dropped the weights. They rolled—and kept coming and coming and coming. I barely got out in time or I would have been crushed. As I rather dazedly began shooting again, I caught this world record lift.

Nikkormat EL with an 85mm f1.8 lens, Kodachrome film and strobe lighting.

23. One of the most visual aspects of sport has always been defeat. Defeat for some reason lends itself almost as well as victory to good photographs. This picture was taken at the Mexico City 1968 Summer Olympic Games and shows an English relay team which had come in last in the finals of the 100 meter relay.

300mm lens, Ektachrome film.

24. During the running of the 3,000 meter Steeplechase Race, you can always be sure to find the largest crowd of photographers gathered around the water jump. It always makes the best pictures. In order to get a different picture of the water jump, I mounted a remote control camera just beneath the hurdle in front of the water jump, and fired it as the runners leaped over. This picture was taken during the final elimination in the United States Olympic Trials at Eugene, Oregon, in 1972. The winners of this race went on to compete for the United States in the Munich Olympic Games.

17mm f3.5 Takumar lens, Kodachrome film.

25. Dick Butkus was a great linebacker with the Chicago Bears and, possibly, the best player I've seen in the game. I took this picture as part of an essay on Butkus and the idea was to try somehow to capture the feeling of playing against him. I used a very long lens and my hope was to catch a moment when only Butkus was in the picture and the photograph gave the effect of being the guy Butkus was about to tackle.

1000mm f5.6 Zeiss lens, Kodachrome 64 ASA film.

26. Occasionally, you find a subject that makes good photographs regardless of whether he's in the game, sitting on the bench or sitting in his car. Joe Namath is that sort of an athlete. This picture was taken during a muddy afternoon at Shea Stadium. There were only a couple of minutes left in the game, and the Jets were two touchdowns behind and Joe was still trying to win it with some help from his upstairs coaches.

While every photographer complains about the kind of weather this picture was taken in, it usually makes for good pictures, ones that a photographer remembers years and years after those taken on beautiful days are forgotten. But pictures like this are becoming more and more rare as stadiums adopt synthetic turf rather than real grass—the playing surface they still have at Shea Stadium.

50mm lens, high speed Ektachrome daylight film.

27. In his own game, Burt Reynolds is every bit the superstar that Joe Namath is in football. Burt was a fine college player and when the opportunity came to act a prisoner-quarterback in the movie *The Longest Yard* Burt jumped at the chance. To a sports photographer, shooting a film version of football was a pleasure. Instead of wondering and hoping that the play would go where I had my camera focused, I knew the plays in advance. And most of the time, plays were run over and over again. It provided some of the best football pictures I'd ever taken. This photograph was posed late one afternoon while the final scene was being filmed.

300mm f2.8 lens, Kodachrome film.

28. Undoubtedly, Muhammad Ali is the most famous athlete in the world today. For the photographer, Ali is a dream. I've been lucky to have had a number of opportunities to photograph Muhammad both in action and in posed situations. This picture was taken just before the Jerry Quarry fight, in which Ali was making a comeback after a three and a half year layoff. I took it after a training session in Miami at the Fifth Street Gym. It was a typical Ali session. He said, "Hurry up, I've only got five minutes" and when I showed him the first Polaroid, he said, "God, I look pretty." An hour later, he was still posing. Ali liked this photograph so much that he used it as his official picture, the one he gives away for autographs.

85mm lens and strobe lighting.

29. While Muhammad Ali was certainly the most famous human athlete of my era, there is no question that Secretariat was the most famous horse. This picture was taken as Secretariat won the 1973 Kentucky Derby. By using a long lens and mounting the camera under the top infield rail, I hoped to capture the feeling that Secretariat was running straight at the viewer. (In fact, the camera was about 100 feet from the finish line.) This is the sort of picture I try every year at the Derby. It works about one out of three times. Needless to say, when I saw this shot, I knew it had worked best of all.

The second most enjoyable part about this win of Secretariat's was that it was one of the rare Derbys when I had money on the right horse.

300mm f2.8 lens, 64 ASA Ektachrome film.

30. Anyone who has been to an Olympic Games will tell you that one of the most exciting things to see is the winning of a gold medal by a countryman. Watching the national flag being raised and listening to the anthem is a thrill one can never forget. When the winner of the event happens to be a close friend of yours, that makes it all the more enjoyable. In Munich, Frank Shorter was the favorite to win the Marathon Run. Frank had been a friend of mine for two or three years and, in fact, had been my assistant during the Pan-American Games in Cali, Colombia. He ran a 10,000 meters and a marathon in Cali but between races, carried my cameras and was one of the best assistants I'd ever had. He and I became good friends. As the Marathon began in Munich, I could hardly wait for the finish of the race. A photographer has to remain detached but in this particular race, my interest was strong. I took this picture to get a view of the entire field at the beginning of the race and I hoped all along that I would be able to take a picture framed exactly the same way showing Frank winning the race.

180mm lens, high speed Ektachrome film.

31. This picture was taken just over two hours after the previous one. As I had hoped all along, Frank came into the stadium all by himself. The only thing I worried about in taking it was that I would be calm enough to keep the focus sharp. Frank came across the finish line with a winning grin on his face and no one could have been happier than I. My hope had been that the two pictures would match perfectly: one showing the huge field and the other showing the lone winner. I think that the result proves the point.

32

33

34

35

36

37

38

39

40

41

32. This photograph was made during the Wimbledon Men's Final in 1976. Bjorn Borg was playing Ilie Nastase and for a photographer this was a match with special interest. Nastase had spent the entire week giving photographers the finger and throwing towels or shouting obscenities. It was a pleasure therefore to see Bjorn Borg tear him apart.

300mm f2.8 lens, Ektachrome 64 ASA film.

33. Reggie Jackson is one of those ballplayers who has a charisma that creates good pictures whether he is hitting a home run or striking out. As Red Smith points out, this picture was taken just after Reggie had a third strike called on him. I had always found Reggie one of the most pleasant ballplayers to deal with. He has a very good understanding of the job of the photographer, and he tries his best to make it easy on most of us. Or at least, he has with me. After the strike-out, however, Reggie came into the dugout and was glaring over at the photographers' box. He was furious because it was his second or third strikeout in the game. He took his helmet off and flung it in the direction of the helmet rack which was right below where I was shooting from. His aim was a little high, though, and the helmet sailed about two feet over my head. After the game, I went into the locker room to ask Reggie why he'd thrown his helmet at me. He looked surprised, and said that he had just thrown his helmet out of frustration. He reminded me that he was an amateur photographer and that I had been giving him film for a couple of years and that he would never throw a helmet at me and cut off his film supply.

500mm f5 mirror lens, high speed Ektachrome film.

34. Most of the action photography done by sports photographers is done with a sequence camera. The hope is usually to pick one key moment out of the sequence that becomes the main picture. This picture was taken during the controversial play at the plate which involved Steve Garvey and Thurman Munson during the 1977 World Series. It was an unusual sequence for me in that every single picture in the sequence would have been worth using. First there was the tag at the plate, then Garvey starting to get up (as this picture shows) screaming at the umpire who had called him out. When he got up, the umpire came into the picture and there was the classic confrontation between player and umpire. An interesting sidelight is that Munson is still standing with the ball holding the tag on Garvey's thigh.

400mm f3.5 lens, Ektachrome EPD film pushed to 800 ASA.

35. The best baseball story of the early 1972 season was Willie Mays' return to New York. Having been a Brooklyn Dodger fan as a kid, I was never very happy about Willie Mays. But when I became a professional photographer, Willie was a favorite of mine. Any picture you took of Willie turned out well. He looked good when he was swinging a bat, chasing a fly ball or running the bases. Shooting portraits of Willie, one could never miss. He always had that great smile that beams out of this portrait.

105mm lens, Ektachrome 64 ASA film.

36. If I had to, I'm not sure that I could pick a personal favorite of my photographs in this book. But I am certain this would be one of the top three. As I mentioned earlier, this picture proves the point that bad weather is probably the sport photographer's best friend. I'll never forget this day in November of 1962. The game began in pouring rain which changed to sleet late in the second half. I took this picture minutes before the game ended. It shows Sam Huff, star linebacker of the early 1960s Giant team, going back on the field for the final plays of the game.

50mm lens, high speed Ektachrome daylight film.

37. The FA Cup Final is to English soccer fans what the Super Bowl is to American football fans. This picture was taken during Arsenal's win over Liverpool in the 1971 FA Cup Final at Wembley Stadium. When I arrived in England, *Sports Illustrated* was told by the FA Cup Final organizers that they could not have a pass for me. They said the game had so many photo requests that they could only handle English photographers. As it turned out, some of my friends from ABC Television's *Wide World of Sports* invited me to dinner two or three nights before the game and they had with them a retired soccer player named Danny Blanchflower who was to do the color commentary of the match on the air. I had never heard of Danny but it turned out that he was the Joe DiMaggio of English soccer. I told him of my troubles getting an on-field pass and he said, "Don't worry about a thing." On the day of the Final I went to the stadium with Danny; it was quite an experience. People would beep their horns on the highway and wave at Danny since his face is familiar to every English soccer fan.

When we got to the stadium, he took me by the arm and simply walked me out onto the field, found somebody who had an extra pass, and solved my problem.

180mm lens, Ektachrome 64 ASA film.

38. Since most major American sports events occur on weekends, it is unusual for a sports photographer to spend the weekend at home. In the fall, when the football season is just beginning, it almost never happens. But what do you think a sports photographer like myself does when he has a Sunday at home? On a particular Sunday morning in October 1977, like many fathers, I went to photograph my six-year-old son Corey playing in a kid's soccer league, near our home in Dix Hills, New York. Corey is the little guy in the middle with the light-green shirt, chasing the ball. And once he sees the picture in this book there'll be no stopping him.

200mm f4 lens, Kodachrome film.

39. Another example of why bad weather makes such wonderful pictures. I took this picture of the 18th green at Augusta during a rainy afternoon in the Masters Golf Tournament of 1975. Getting a seat at 18 is a very difficult thing to do. One has to arrive very early and not dare to leave because if you do, you never get back in the crowd. Therefore, when the rain came, a sea of beautifully colored umbrellas opened up and the fans—myself included—just sat and watched as long as the players continued playing.

Nikkormat EL camera, 24mm lens, high speed Ektachrome daylight film.

40. Here is the photographer's perfect winter assignment. I took this picture during the 1977 Hawaiian Open in Honolulu: it shows Tom Watson on the fairway just about to hit to the green. The least bit of noise bothers golfers and it is very difficult to take a picture of a golfer midway through his backswing. In order to make this shot, I worked from far away with a long lens and made exposures one by one rather than using the noisier motor-driven sequence camera.

500mm f5 mirror lens, Ektachrome 64 ASA.

41. Jack Nicklaus is definitely among those athletes with photographic charisma. In Jack's case, however, he has an added ingredient that none of the others have: Jack has a caddy with

42

43

44

45

46

47

48

49

charisma. I took this picture on the 16th green in Augusta just after Jack had sunk a long birdie putt in the 1972 Masters Golf Tournament, which he went on to win.

500mm f5 mirror lens, Ektachrome 64 ASA film.

42. One of the nicest things about sports photography is that one usually gets to see an event from the best seat in the house. This picture of the Australian 12-meter boat *Dame Pattie* during the 1967 America's Cup Races in Newport, Rhode Island, is a perfect example. I got to watch the entire race from a Goodyear blimp. Other than the fact that it didn't have a restaurant, there could be no better place to see the race. You avoided the traffic on the water, the ride was smooth, it was equally impossible to get seasick or airsick, and I enjoyed every minute of it.

105mm lens, Kodachrome film.

43. Sunset is always one of the prettiest times of the day to take pictures. The problem with shooting sunset pictures is that you can't control the weather. I waited two or three days for the right kind of day in order to shoot this picture of an iceboat at sunset in Green Lake, Wisconsin. Beginning about half an hour before sunset, I positioned myself about 100 yards away from the boat with a very long lens and waited. The sun sank lower and lower and I kept my fingers crossed that it wouldn't get behind a thin layer of clouds that was on the horizon; sure enough, everything worked perfectly. What I hadn't counted on, however, was that just about the time I was ready to shoot, I had also become nearly frostbitten. I have never been so cold in my life but the excitement of the sun being exactly where I wanted it and the iceboat being just where I wanted was enough to make me forget the cold temporarily. I shot a set of pictures and quickly got off the lake.

1000mm lens, Kodachrome film.

44. In order to shoot pictures that showed the speed and excitement of iceboating, I knew that I had to ride one; also, there was no way to attach a remote camera where I wanted it. The iceboat that I shot from had a small kyack-type seat in front of the mast. I positioned myself in it and off we went. It took a few rides before I got up enough courage to keep from holding on. Once I got my hands on my camera, I just focused on the driver and waited for the runner plank to lift off

the ice in what is called the hiking position. This picture was taken on Lake Geneva, Wisconsin.

24mm lens, Kodakchrome film.

45. To determine the running order for skiers in a major race, the field is broken into seeds of 15. The best skiers are placed in the first seed. The order of running is then drawn out of a hat. Obviously, the ideal spot to run is in the middle of the field. The most difficult spot to run would be number 15 because all the pressure is on this skier since he knows the results of those who ran the course before. During the 1976 Winter Olympics at Innsbruck, the favorite to win the downhill—the most glamorous race in all skiing—was Franz Klammer. Being a native Austrian put particular pressure on Klammer. When I tried to figure out where to position myself to photograph his downhill run, I felt that the start would best capture the tension and excitement. This picture was taken just before Klammer began his gold medal–winning run.

300mm f5.6 lens, Ektachrome 64 ASA film.

46. The setting for the 70 meter ski jump in Sapporo, Japan, for the 1972 Winter Olympic Games was as beautiful as any I'd ever seen. I decided that instead of taking a picture that showed what a jumper looked like, I wanted to try to take a picture that showed what the ski jump looked like to the skier. I positioned myself at the top of the run and shot from behind the skier, looking down into the town of Sapporo. This picture was actually shot in 1971, not during the Olympics, but a year earlier when the Japanese held the rehearsal for the 1972 Games.

24mm lens, Kodachrome film.

47. For me, this picture represents a dream. I am at best an intermediate skier. What I most want to do one day is ski a run like the one in this photograph. It is called Limelight, is at Sun Valley, and is one of the most difficult mogul runs in the world. I took the picture late in the afternoon when the shadows were long and therefore accentuated the height of the moguls. I waited as skiers descended through the bumps. The run was sufficiently treacherous so that not many skiers tried it that afternoon. I spent about an hour and got a number of groups of skiers going down, including the one in the picture; they almost succeeded in making it all the way in one

run. I then put on my skis and continued down the beginner run on the hill across the valley from Limelight.

400mm f5.6 lens, Kodachrome film.

48. This picture was part of an essay I shot before the 1972 Munich Olympic Games showing America's best hopes in women's diving. This is Micki King, who was to go on to win a gold medal in platform diving. I wanted to make it clear that she was diving from more than 30 feet up, but while shooting I realized that I had lost the feeling of height because I was looking down onto flat, calm water. I couldn't tell whether she was diving from three meters, five meters or ten meters. In order to solve the problem, I filled the swimming pool with kids, and the scale of their faces ten meters below told the story. Then I got on a ladder above Micki, and had her dive just below me. This was one of the most frightening moments of my career, because the momentum of Micki's dive carried her outward and I had to lean way forward. The ladder came perilously close to falling into the pool. It took five minutes to get my heart back to normal but when I saw the pictures, I knew it had been worth it.

The picture was taken with a Hulcher sequence camera which takes up to 50 frames per second. I used a 35mm Nikon lens and Kodachrome film.

49. Big surfing waves hit the north shore of Hawaii about 6 or 7 times a year, but with the greatest frequency in December or January. Just when you're going to get a perfect day is impossible to predict. The big-wave surfers don't waste their time on anything but the best waves—20- to 25-footers. They've developed a system of letting each other know when the surf is up. At about four o'clock in the morning, a chain of phone calls goes from surfer to surfer, each one calling the next to let him know whether the surf is up. The ten days I was in Hawaii, I would get a call every morning about four. Bleary-eyed, I'd wake up and someone would tell me that the surf was not up. I then had to call the next person on my list, after which I went back to sleep for a while and enjoyed Hawaii for another day. Finally, the right day came. I was told that the surf was to be terrific that day. I headed out to the north shore where Sports Illustrated had arranged a helicopter for me. The rest was a snap: I just hung up there over the waves and shot roll after roll of film. The surfers spent from sunrise to sunset riding the big waves.

24mm lens, Kodachrome.

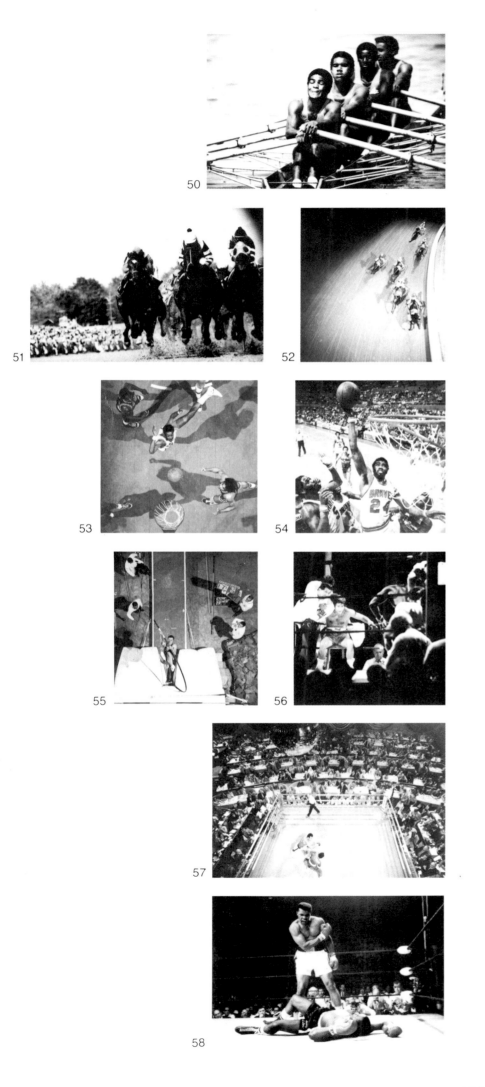

50. The thing I've always liked about this picture, which I took in Mexico City at the 1975 Pan-American Games, is the different expressions on each of the faces of the Cuban rowing team. Despite the fact that they're in exactly the same moment of the race, the man in front looks magnificent—he's a photographer's dream—but the oarsman in back seems bored to death.

400mm f5.6 lens, Kodachrome film.

51. I guess I've just got good luck when it comes to Triple Crown winners. As I pointed out in the Secretariat picture, when one puts the camera under the rail at the Kentucky Derby, you'll usually succeed one out of three times. Well, I've only succeeded twice. The first time it produced the picture of Secretariat and the second time was when I shot this picture of Seattle Slew at the 1977 Derby. This shot was made as Seattle Slew passed the finish line, by the grandstand the first time, still having a mile to go.

300mm f5.6 lens, and Ektachrome 64 ASA film.

52. Most sports photographers today are wedded to their motor-driven or sequence cameras. But many old-timers compare taking pictures with the sequence cameras as against the Speed Graphic, say, to the difference between hunting with a bow and arrow or a machine gun. They like to say, "How can you miss, after all, you can shoot dozens of pictures in one second. In the old days, we had only one chance." I'm particularly pleased with this picture which I took during the 1968 running of the Roosevelt Raceway International because it was a throwback to the old days. I had only one chance. The picture was taken with a remote camera mounted above the final turn at the raceway track and it was synchronized to a series of strobe lights. The horses would pass this spot twice but it was the second time that I wanted for the picture. You have only one chance in this kind of situation and when it works as well as it did here, it's a particularly pleasing result.

The picture was taken with a motorized Hasselblad camera fired remotely and synchronized to a set of Ascor strobe units.

53. A sports photographer is always looking for a different way of shooting the same game. As the season progresses, one gets more and more tired of seeing basketball pictures taken from beneath the basket. I decided to photograph the

180

ACC Basketball Championships of 1976 from the ceiling directly above the basket. Aside from getting a slightly stiff neck, I surely had the best seat in the house and the pictures were great.

Hasselblad camera, 350mm lens, Ektachrome film and strobe lighting.

54. Another example of a different view of basketball—this picture was taken with a camera mounted directly behind the Plexiglas backboard right at rim level. My greatest anxiety about this picture was whether the camera would survive the pre-game warm-up when each player seemed to make it his personal obligation to see if he could shake the camera loose. I kept my fingers crossed during the entire warm-up and then just sat beneath the basket and fired the camera every time I thought the players were in the right spot. It's a very exciting thing for a photographer to do this kind of photography because you really can't visualize exactly what the camera saw since you weren't looking through it.

Hasselblad motor-driven camera with a 50mm lens, Ektachrome film and strobe lighting.

55. As in the case of the previous two basketball pictures, this one is simply the result of my wanting to photograph the pole vault in a different way. It was taken during the AAU National Championships in 1966 in Albuquerque, New Mexico. I positioned myself in the catwalk directly above the pole vault and waited for each vaulter to come down the runway. When they were looking straight up at me, I shot the picture. This photograph shows Bob Seagren setting a world record of 17 feet ¼ inch. I particularly like this kind of picture because I was able to include the scoreboard showing the numbers—irrefutable facts that demonstrate that this was the world record vault and no other.

Hasselblad camera, 250mm lens and strobe lighting.

56. The second Nino Benvenuti–Emile Griffith fight was held outdoors at Shea Stadium in September of 1967. In it, Griffith regained his title from the Italian champion, who had taken it from Griffith only five months before. In turn, Benvenuti took the title back from Griffith in March, 1968. When I got to the stadium to look for a position to shoot from, I noticed that it was a particularly good opportunity to photograph a fight from a position other than my usual ringside

seat. Instead of sitting in the front row this time, I positioned myself back about 40 feet from the ring against one of the support pillars that held the overhead ring lighting setup. My intention here was to capture the excitement sensed as the fighters answer the bell for a round in the fight. The fighter is tense particularly when the fight is close and I thought that getting away from ringside and being able to pull in the two fighters with a long lens would catch this feeling much better than a ringside picture might have done. I backlit Benvenuti's corner with a red filter on the strobe light to add a little more drama.

Hasselblad camera with a 500mm lens and strobe lighting. The strobes were mounted over the ring.

57. As soon as I arrived in Lake Tahoe for the 1972 Muhammad Ali–Bob Foster fight, I knew exactly how to photograph it. The setting was unreal. I'd seen Ali fight about 20 times before, but I'd never seen anything like this. The ring was right in the middle of a nightclub. I mounted the camera above the ring and my objective was to capture the action below but include the entire scene behind the ring. The one thing about this picture that's always bothered me is that I have had to fill dozens of requests for prints from people who've spotted themselves in the background. For weeks after it appeared someone else would call and say, "Listen, I'm the guy in the red coat in the fourth row. I saw your picture of Ali-Foster, how can I get a print of it?" I must have made about 50 prints.

24mm lens; the entire arena was strobe lit with overhead strobes.

58. Undoubtedly my best-known picture is this one of Muhammad Ali, then Cassius Clay, standing over Sonny Liston after his first-round knockout in the World Championship fight at Lewiston, Maine, in May 1965. It is the best example I can give of good luck and perfect execution. Needless to say, I'm the luckiest guy at ringside since Ali is staring straight at me. As Red Smith pointed out in his Foreword, all you have to do is look between Ali's legs to see the other Sports Illustrated photographer Herb Scharfman and you realize just how lucky I was. On the other hand, this was a single shot picture; I had only one chance and the execution of this situation is what I'm most proud of. The lighting was carefully planned. I used overhead strobe lights and I feel that part of the success of the picture is that the lighting enhanced the drama of the situation.

When Liston fell, I was probably the only person in the arena who was praying he wouldn't get up. I knew I already had as good a picture as I could possibly get in the fight. And this is probably the best-known picture of Ali fighting; I've been trying to get one nearly as good ever since then with very little success.

Rolleiflex wide-angle camera, Ektachrome film and strobe lighting.

59. Of all the people I've met in the world of sports, Joe Frazier may be the nicest. He is that rare superstar who genuinely seems to care about the people around him. Every time I see Joe, he makes a point of asking how my family is, how I am, how business is, and when Joe asks, he has a sincerity about him that makes you know he really cares. The fight in Manila may have been the most exciting fight I've ever covered. This picture, which was taken at the press conference following the fight, is one of the most difficult I've ever shot. I liked Joe so much that it really hurt to look at his face after the beating he had taken. His courage that day is something I don't think I'll ever forget. Almost all my experience of photographing boxing has been pleasant. I genuinely like the sport. This is one of the few pictures of boxing that I really didn't enjoy making.

Nikkormat camera with an 85mm lens, high speed Ektachrome type B film and television lighting.

60. Almost as charismatic as Ali himself, Don King is a pleasure to photograph. How can you miss: the hair, the face, the ever-present cigar and tux. The only mistake Don and I made when I took this picture was that he wore all his jewelry. After the picture appeared in *Sports Illustrated*, Don was afraid to wear the watch, the ring, any of the diamonds, because the magazine had pointed out that they were worth over a hundred thousand dollars and Don suddenly became aware of the fact that he was a natural target for mugging. I used a black background in this picture, which was taken in a studio, so that by backlighting Don I would emphasize the smoke from his cigar.

Hasselblad, 150mm lens and studio lighting on Ektachrome film.

61. From a personal standpoint, probably my favorite picture in the book would be this picture of President Ford skiing in Vail, Colorado. It is the

only picture that was taken specifically to be used in this book. My intention was to show that even presidents relax through sport. I took the picture in December 1975 when Ford was still president. Being a great Gerald Ford fan myself, I hoped he would still be in office for at least five more years. When I called David Kennerly, the White House photographer, and asked if I could spend the day skiing with the President, he informed me that the President was in Vail on vacation and that this was the one time when they tried to let him relax without being surrounded by photographers. I pointed out to him that this picture would not be for publication in the magazine but was solely for use in the book I was preparing on my photographs. He went to the President and to my surprise my trip was approved. I decided to insure my chances by calling an old friend, the great ski racer Billy Kidd, and asking if he would assist me. When the President met us, it turned out that he was as eager to ski with Billy as Billy was to ski with the President. I needed Billy to carry the cameras, but when the President asked if it would be possible to borrow Billy for the run, I could not say no. They headed for the ski lift. Billy, who was America's only gold medal winner in World Ski Championship, was also a silver medalist in the Innsbruck Olympics of 1964. Billy and the President skied two runs and when they reached me the second time the President asked if I had had enough pictures for the day. I thanked him and said I had, at which point he asked me if I didn't want to ski the final run of the day with him. It hurt me to say so but I looked up at him and said, "Mr. President, you're skiing much too well for me and I would only slow you down." We shook hands. It was one of the most enjoyable sporting days of my career.

200mm f4 lens, Kodachrome film.

62. Rumors were very strong that if the Green Bay Packers won the 1968 Super Bowl against the Oakland Raiders, the famed Packer coach, Vince Lombardi, would retire and move into the front office as General Manager. As the final seconds of the game ticked away with the Packers well in front, Lombardi became the prime target of every photographer on the sidelines. I'm particularly proud of this picture because all photographers at the end of a game try to maneuver in front of the winning coach as he is carried off the field. I waited as the seconds ticked away and when the gun went off, I was standing right in front of Vince with all the other photographers pretty well behind me. This picture appeared on the cover of *Sports Illustrated* and has been one of my favorites.

24mm lens, high speed Ektachrome daylight film.

63. The objective in this picture of Floyd Patterson fighting Jerry Quarry was to try to make the camera seem to be the eyes of one of the fighters. I wanted to try to capture what a weary fighter must see late in a fight as he looks at his opponent. I smeared Vaseline on a clear filter across the lens to blur the overhead strobes on which I had put colored filters to add to the drama.

Hasselblad camera, 50mm lens, Ektachrome film and overhead strobe lighting.

64. If anyone ever wanted to do a handbook on how to ride race horses, this picture would be a perfect example. It shows the great Willie Shoemaker riding Northern Dancer to victory in the Florida Derby of 1964. In this particular race, instead of betting with money, I bet my camera. The finish line at Gulfstream Race Track was fully covered by shadows when the race was to be run but the quarter pole, a quarter of a mile from the finish, was in bright sun. I knew the horses and the colors on the jockeys' silks would be much prettier if I shot there. I gambled, and sure enough, when Northern Dancer passed me he was already in the lead. He never relinquished that lead, so the picture I shot was just as valid as if I had worked at the finish line.

The picture was taken with a 70mm Hulcher camera, 300mm astro lens and Ektachrome 70mm daylight film.

65 and 66. These are two examples of the kind of football photography I like to do. The top picture was taken on a muddy day at Shea Stadium and happens to show the winning catch in the Jets' victory that day. The bottom picture was taken during the 1977 Rose Bowl and captures the frustration that Michigan suffered.

Both pictures were taken with 300mm f2.8 lens and Ektachrome film.

67. Another example of why photographers hate fields with synthetic turf. Mud makes great pictures. This one was taken late in a game at Shea Stadium and shows one of the Buffalo Bill linesmen trying to get a bit of nourishment.

180mm lens, high speed Ektachrome daylight film.

me. Al Schneider of the Life Photo Lab had converted a 250 exposure Nikon camera into a photo finish type camera (others would call it a strip or slit camera). The camera operates on the principle that the film and the subject pass by a slit in opposite directions and if the speed of the film is the same as the speed of the subject, you get an honest reporting of the subject. Here, the car is frozen perfectly but the blurred ground reflects the high speed. If the speed of the film and the subject were different, you would either get an elongated or a compressed racing car.

This picture was taken on Kodachrome film with the special strip camera and a 105mm lens.

80. The perfect sports picture is the one that shows the key player in the key moment of the game in a great photograph. Clay standing over Liston, Secretariat barreling down the stretch are two of my best examples. This is a third. It was taken at Shea Stadium in December of 1973 and shows O.J. Simpson at the very instant he broke the long-held NFL rushing record of Jimmy Brown. O.J. got closer and closer to the record during the game and I kept hoping that on his record run he would run toward my side of the field. On the few runs that preceded this one he went the other way and I had no chance. I couldn't believe it when with just about four yards to go to break the record, O.J. turned the corner and headed straight toward my camera. This picture is an example of good execution and luck at its best.

300mm f2.8 lens, high speed Ektachrome.

81. If you think I was lucky in the O.J. Simpson picture, can you imagine what the odds must have been to get this picture of Ron Turcotte looking straight over at me just before he crossed the finish line in his winning ride of Secretariat to capture the Belmont Stakes and become the first Triple Crown winner in over 25 years. I've never quite figured out exactly what it was about me and Secretariat, but he certainly was the luckiest horse for me I've ever photographed. While he won the Triple Crown on the track, I won it with my camera.

Since racing is the kind of sport that you'll always miss just because the horse runs on the wrong part of the track, I couldn't believe my luck when I succeeded in getting a wonderful picture of Secretariat winning the Derby, a classic of Secretariat turning for home in the Preakness and then this picture of Secretariat just as he claims the Belmont and Triple Crown. I think if I cover horse racing for another 50 years, I'll never get that lucky again with one horse in three straight races.

300mm f2.8 lens, Ektachrome film.

82. No, this photograph was not taken during a Roller Derby. This is a look at the sport of the future as depicted in Norman Jewison's film *Rollerball*. This was a savage game in which the scoreboard not only listed goals but injuries and deaths. This shot captures the sport just as Norman had intended it to look on the screen. With the amount of violence on the current sport scene, the movie was, of course, meant as a comment and a kind of warning that such a scene as this should never occur in real sport.

105mm lens, Ektachrome film, movie lighting.

83. As Red Smith points out in his Foreword, the camera is perfectly capable of lying. If you look closely at this picture, you would assume that the Oakland Raiders were having a rough day against the Minnesota Vikings in the 1977 Super Bowl. Of course, just the opposite was true but this particular picture was one of my favorites from the day's shooting.

600mm f5.6 lens, Ektachrome film.

84. Using long lenses enables the photographer to put himself almost into the middle of a game. I took this picture of Minnesota Viking quarterback Fran Tarkenton in 1961 when both Tarkenton and the Vikings were very young and were not yet the super team that they became. It seemed that on every other play, Tarkenton's defense would break down and he would get clobbered and I wanted to get the feeling of what it was like to be a young quarterback in the NFL and survive. I positioned myself in the end zone and waited for Tarkenton to drop back to pass. And just as I said before, on every other play, at least half the Detroit Lion team would get to them. This particular picture was the best of the group.

400mm lens, high speed Ektachrome film.

85. I took this picture while working on an essay on the older players in the NFL. Each man I photographed had played at least 15 years. Charlie Krueger of the San Francisco '49ers was my favorite. Charlie had a face like every pug you've ever seen, complete with cauliflower ear. At the moment I shot this portrait, he had just come out of the game after having gotten his bell rung.

300mm f2.8 lens, Kodachrome film.

86. In his own way, Jackie Stewart's face is as interesting as Casey Stengel's. I felt that every bit of tension that a race driver must feel shows when you look really closely at Jackie's face. What I wanted to do in this picture, taken before the running of the French Grand Prix in 1973, was to come in close to capture the intensity and concentration of a world champion Grand Prix race driver.

180mm lens, Kodachrome film.

87. Mark Spitz is certainly one of the best-known athletes of our time. In order to take a portrait of him different from all others I'd seen, I asked Mark if he would lie on his back in the pool and submerge his face just beneath the surface of the water. He was to create as little ripple as possible. As you can see, he followed instructions.

105mm lens, Kodachrome film.

88. During the 1976 Winter Olympics in Innsbruck, I tried an experiment—to make a shot I'd always wanted to get with slalom skiing. I ran one roll of film through the camera on the entire second group of racers (none of them likely to turn up winners). Then, double exposed the same roll of film against the crowd in the background. I think the picture is one of the best I've shot at the Olympic Games.

Both pictures were taken with a 200mm f4 lens.

89. No, your eyes are not fooling you. These skiers are indeed using only one ski. This is a sport called monoskiing. Because of its difficulty it's unlikely that it will ever catch on. I shot this picture by lying flat in the snow just downhill from a bump. As the skiers began their run, they would yell, "Here we come" and I would start the camera going and they'd jump right over me.

The picture was made with a Hulcher 35mm sequence camera with a 15mm Nikon lens on Kodachrome film.

90. Every heavyweight boxer dreams of getting a shot at the title. For Chuck Wepner, his chance came against Muhammad Ali in 1975. Unfortunately, Wepner had fought too many ring wars before: he was known as the Bayone Bleeder.

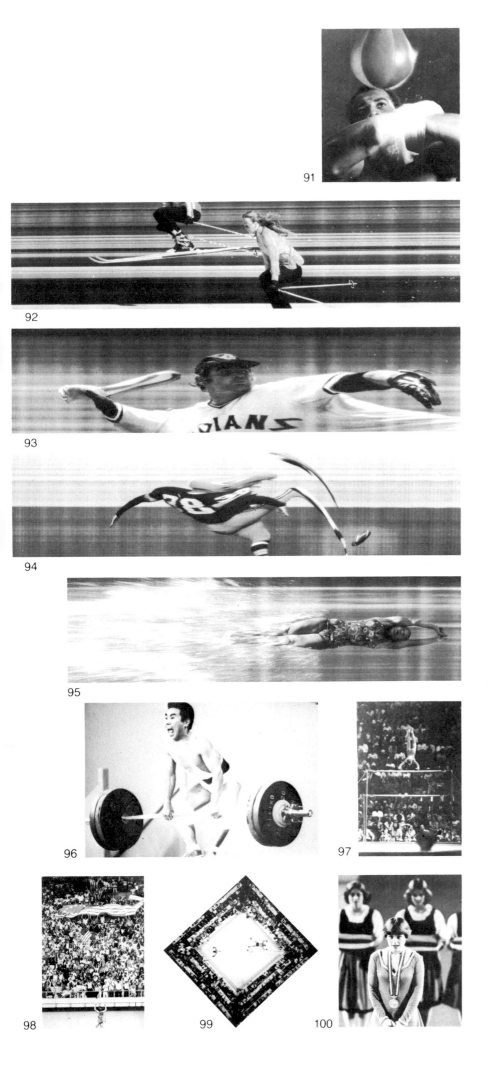

His defense in the ring was never quite as big as his heart and he ended up catching a lot more punches than he ever gave. His face showed it. In fact, the actor-writer Sylvester Stallone got his idea for the movie *Rocky* from watching the Wepner-Ali fight. I gave Stallone a copy of this picture and his first comment was, "Yup, that's it, that's Rocky."

The portrait was taken with a Synar 4x5 camera, Ektachrome film and strobe lighting. It was posed; the "sweat" on Wepner's face is water that I put there.

91. I probably photographed 50 fighters hitting the speed bag, but I never really succeeded in getting a good picture. The bag always seemed to be in the wrong place; either there was an ugly background or a pillar in the way or some other reason why I couldn't get a good picture. I wanted to photograph Ken Norton hitting the speed bag and decided to try to do it in the studio. The boxing equipment people from Everlast were kind enough to build me a speed bag in the studio and that created a perfect situation. I was able to control the background and the lighting and took this picture of Ken Norton just prior to his title fight against Muhammad Ali in 1976 at Yankee Stadium. The photo session was a long one and when Norton finished he told me that I may have given him the best workout that he'd had for the fight.

Hasselblad camera, 150mm lens, Ektachrome film and studio strobe lighting.

92-95. Although these pictures are of different sports—skiing, baseball, football and diving—the technique is exactly the same in each. This is another use of the strip camera I described earlier. In each instance, the subject—the skiers, Gaylord Perry pitching, the girl diver or the football player—passed in front of the slit and recorded themselves as they and the film traveled in opposite directions. The reason for the distortion in the pictures of pitcher and football player is that the speed at which the subjects passed the slit differed from the speed at which the film was passing in the opposite direction.

All pictures were shot with a Nikon F 250mm camera converted into a photo finish camera. The skier, football player and diver were taken with a 105mm lens; the baseball player was taken with a 1000mm Zeiss f5.6 lens.

96. Having done an essay on the super heavyweight

weight lifters, I was really excited about the prospect of seeing the little guys during the 1976 Summer Olympic Games at Montreal. They proved to be as exciting to watch as anything I saw in Montreal; this picture of a Japanese weight lifter was one of my best taken in the entire Games.

300mm f2.8 lens, Ektachrome EPD 200 speed film pushed 2 stops to 800 ASA. (All indoor pictures at the 1976 Olympic Games were shot on daylight film because the television lighting used in the stadium was balanced for daylight.)

97. There are some events that I can't quite figure out how to do properly, no matter how often I photograph them. The uneven bars in the Olympics looked beautiful, but I've never quite figured out exactly how to photograph them. This picture is as close as I've come to success. It shows Olga Korbut during the 1976 Olympic Games. Normally, I would have been right up next to the uneven bars to shoot this picture. But I had selected a spot on the opposite side of the arena in order to keep what I thought would be the best position to photograph the most beautiful of all women's gymnastic events, the balance beam. So I finally got my picture of the uneven bars from right beneath the balance beam shooting all the way across the arena.

400mm f3.5 lens, high speed Ektachrome EPD 200 speed film pushed 2 stops.

98. Certainly the most memorable American victory in Montreal was that of Bruce Jenner winning the Decathlon. The picture of Jenner crossing the finish line with his arms in the air has appeared in nearly every newspaper and magazine and even on the cover of the Wheaties box of cereal. But I chose this picture as my favorite because it shows Jenner in a completely different moment—as he runs his victory lap following the 1500 meter event in the Decathlon. I took it as Jenner passed under a large American contingent seated on the far side of the track and I feel it captures the mood of an Olympic victory.

300mm f2.8 lens, Ektachrome EPD 200 speed film.

99. From time to time in these captions, I refer to the importance of luck in making great sports pictures. But this picture represents the luckiest moment I've ever had in sports photography. For the Cleveland Williams–Muhammad Ali World Championship fight, I set a camera in a gondola that was lowered from the roof of the Houston Astrodome until it was about 50 feet above the ring. My intention was to get a picture of the loser (I was sure it would be Williams) stretched out on his back looking up at the camera. And I hoped to capture the victor with his arms in the air in victory. I hoped for the picture to be perfectly symmetrical and my biggest worry was the two microphones that hung down from the gondola. One of them might obscure one or both of the fighters. Another problem, of course, was that the knockout might occur over in a corner or up against the ropes, which would have ruined the mood and feeling that I was after. Well, one look at this picture and you will see that if I were to try a hundred more times, I doubt that it could happen more perfectly. Ali knocked Williams down, I waited for him to cross the ring until he was on the opposite (neutral) corner and clicked this picture. Needless to say, I couldn't wait to see the film.

The photograph was taken with a 50mm lens, a Hasselblad motorized camera mounted remotely above the ring and lit with strobe lighting on daylight Ektachrome 64 ASA film.

100. The only difficulty in taking this picture of Dorothy Hamill watching the American flag being raised at the 1976 Olympic Games in Innsbruck was that I'm a fairly sentimental guy and I start shaking and getting goose bumps at a moment like this. I was positioned on a balcony directly in front of the flag. In fact, if I had reached out, I could have touched it. I managed to keep calm as I shot this picture and could see Dorothy looking straight at me.

300mm f2.8 lens, high speed Ektachrome daylight film pushed 2 stops.

Front Endpaper Picture

This picture may look easy, but, in fact, it was one of the most difficult I had to take. The problem here was that in order to get an aerial photograph of Shea Stadium at dusk with Manhattan and its skyline silhouetted against the setting sun, I had to position myself in a helicopter just beyond the outfield wall of Shea Stadium. Normally, that would be no problem—except that the main runway for LaGuardia Airport is directly in line with where the helicopter had to be. I convinced the pilot to try to call the tower people at LaGuardia and he finally talked them into letting us move in and out of the flight path for 15-second intervals. This picture came after three or four tries as an equal number of planes landed safely.

35mm lens, Kodachrome film.

Back Endpaper

The Houston Astrodome is certainly the stadium of the future. I took this picture in 1967 and my intention was to make it look even more futuristic than it is. I did this by shooting both the real stadium and its reflected image in a mirror—which gives it the look of some sort of flying saucer.

35mm lens, Kodachrome type A film.

ACKNOWLEDGMENTS

Wednesday, February 15, 1978 will long be remembered as a very special day in the sports world. It was the night on which Muhammad Ali lost his World Heavyweight Championship to Leon Spinks in Las Vegas, Nevada. While I'll never forget that fight, the day will have a special meaning for me for another reason. The Ali-Spinks fight was the last assignment I shot for *Sports Illustrated* magazine before joining *Time* magazine as a staff photographer.

Since I came to *Sports Illustrated* in 1960 as a 17-year-old kid fresh out of high school, I've spent half my life taking sports pictures and this book is, for me, a dream come true. It contains mostly my best work and in a few instances, my personal favorites. I gave some thought to adding a picture of Spinks' victory to this book, and then decided that what I really wanted to do was to remember Ali the same way I hope to remember my sports pictures...for their best moments, rather than the moments of defeat. That is what this book is all about.

A good photographer cannot do it by himself, and I've certainly been more than fortunate in having help all along the way. I'd like in this brief acknowledgment to thank those people without whom I'd never have been in a position to have my pictures published as they are here. In the beginning, there was Al Silverman, Bob Markel and Paul Durkin, they published my first pictures. Without them, I probably would have gone into another business. *Sports Illustrated* picture editors, Gerald Astor, John Stebbins, George Bloodgood and the late Frank Agolia, gave me the opportunity to literally see the world of sport through my camera. They allowed and encouraged me to continually improve myself and my pictures.

Another mention must be made for the fine assistants I had working with me on so many of my assignments. John Iacono, Manny Millan and Anthony Donna were the three I worked with most. And it's most pleasing to me today to see Johnny, Manny, and occasionally, Anthony shooting pictures for *Sports Illustrated* themselves. Al Schneider of the Life Photo Lab has been invaluable with technical help. Without them, I don't think I could have taken most of these photographs. Managing Editors Andre Laguerre and Roy Terrell published the pictures and their talents made me look awfully good, and I thank them both.

Then came time to try to assemble this book. I had help from Lou Gillenson and Paul Fargas, both of whom made every effort to move this project along and when it arrived at Harry N. Abrams, Inc.—Lena Tabori, Bob Morton and especially, Nai Chang—made sure it was done just right. There is one person without whom, however, this project would never have gotten anywhere, Linda Schwarz, of the *Sports Illustrated* Art Department who helped me for many hours of her own time without any pay to produce a dummy layout of the book that enabled me to get this project off the drawing boards and published. Last but not least, I want to thank my wife, Renae, daughter Jodi, and son Corey. They put up with my being away from home for many, many days, weeks and months at a time. Without them, I don't think I could ever be as successful as I've been.

Neil Leifer